Spies in
the Civil War

THE
CIVIL WAR
A NATION DIVIDED

THE
Civil War
A Nation Divided

Spies in
the Civil War

Heather Lehr Wagner / Consulting Editor **Tim McNeese**

CHELSEA HOUSE
PUBLISHERS
An imprint of Infobase Publishing

SPIES IN THE CIVIL WAR

Copyright © 2009 by Infobase Publishing

Chelsea House
An imprint of Infobase Publishing
132 West 31st Street
New York, NY 10001

Library of Congress Cataloging-in-Publication Data
Wagner, Heather Lehr.
  Spies in the Civil War / by Heather Lehr Wagner.
     p. cm. — (The Civil War : a nation divided)
  Includes bibliographical references and index.
  ISBN 978-1-60413-039-3 (hardcover)
  1. United States—History—Civil War, 1861-1865—Secret service. 2. United States—History—Civil War, 1861-1865—Undergound movements. 3. Spies—United States—History—19th century. 4. Spies—Confederate States of America. 5. Spies—United States—Biography. 6. Spies—Confederate States of America—Biography. I. Title.

  E608.W34 2009
  973.7'86—dc22   2008026568

Series design by Lina Farinella
Cover design by Takeshi Takahashi

Printed in the United States of America

Bang NMSG 10 9 8 7 6 5 4 3 2 1

This book is printed on acid-free paper.

All links and Web addresses were checked and verified to be correct at the time of publication. Because of the dynamic nature of the Web, some addresses and links may have changed since publication and may no longer be valid.

Contents

Chronology

1820   The Missouri Compromise allows Maine to be admitted to the Union as a free state and Missouri as a slave state in 1821.

1831   William Lloyd Garrison publishes the first issue of his abolitionist newspaper, *The Liberator.*

1836   The House of Representatives passes a gag rule that automatically tables or postpones action on all petitions relating to slavery without hearing them.

1838   The Underground Railroad is formally organized.

1845   Former slave Frederick Douglass publishes his autobiography, *Narrative of the Life of Frederick Douglass, An American Slave.*

1850   Congress enacts several measures that together make up the Compromise of 1850.

1852   Harriet Beecher Stowe publishes *Uncle Tom's Cabin.*

1854   Congress passes the Kansas-Nebraska Act, which overturns the Missouri Compromise and thus opens northern territories to slavery.

1855   As Kansas prepares to vote, thousands of Border Ruffians from Missouri enter the territory in an attempt to influence the elections. This begins the period known as Bleeding Kansas.

1856   South Carolina representative Preston Brooks attacks Massachusetts senator Charles Sumner on the Senate floor and beats him with a cane.

1857   The Supreme Court rules, in *Dred Scott v. Sandford*, that blacks are not U.S. citizens and slaveholders have the right to take slaves into free areas of the country.

1859   John Brown seizes the arsenal at Harpers Ferry, Virginia. Robert E. Lee, then a Federal Army regular, leads the troops that capture Brown.

1860   **NOVEMBER**   Abraham Lincoln is elected president.

        DECEMBER   A South Carolina convention passes an ordinance of secession, and the state secedes from the Union.

1861   **JANUARY**   Florida, Alabama, Georgia, and Louisiana secede from the Union.

        FEBRUARY   Texas votes to secede from the Union. The Confederate States of America is formed and elects Jefferson Davis as its president.

        MARCH   Abraham Lincoln is sworn in as the sixteenth president of the United States and delivers his first inaugural address.

        APRIL 12   At 4:30 A.M., Confederate forces fire on South Carolina's Fort Sumter. The Civil War begins. Virginia secedes from the Union five days later.

        MAY   Arkansas and North Carolina secede from the Union.

        JUNE   Tennessee secedes from the Union.

        JULY 21   The Union suffers a defeat in northern Virginia, at the First Battle of Bull Run (Manassas).

        AUGUST   The Confederates win the Battle of Wilson's Creek, in Missouri.

1862   **FEBRUARY 6**   In Tennessee, Union general Ulysses S. Grant captures Fort Henry. Ten days later, he captures Fort Donelson.

MARCH The Confederate ironclad ship CSS *Virginia* (formerly the USS *Merrimack*) battles the Union ironclad *Monitor* to a draw. The Union's Peninsular Campaign begins in Virginia.

APRIL 6–7 Ulysses S. Grant defeats Confederate forces in the Battle of Shiloh (Pittsburg Landing), in Tennessee.

APRIL 24 David Farragut moves his fleet of Union Navy vessels up the Mississippi River to take New Orleans.

MAY 31 The Battle of Seven Pines (Fair Oaks) takes place in Virginia.

JUNE 1 Robert E. Lee assumes command of the Army of Northern Virginia.

JUNE 25–JULY 1 The Seven Days Battles are fought in Virginia.

AUGUST 29–30 The Union is defeated at the Second Battle of Bull Run.

SEPTEMBER 17 The bloodiest day in U.S. military history: Confederate forces under Robert E. Lee are stopped at Antietam, Maryland, by Union forces under George B. McClellan.

SEPTEMBER 22 The first Emancipation Proclamation to free slaves in the rebellious states is issued by President Lincoln.

DECEMBER 13 The Union's Army of the Potomac, under Ambrose Burnside, suffers a costly defeat at Fredericksburg, Virginia.

1863

JANUARY 1 President Lincoln issues the final Emancipation Proclamation.

JANUARY 29 Ulysses S. Grant is placed in command of the Army of the West, with orders to capture Vicksburg, Mississippi.

MAY 1–4   Union forces under Joseph Hooker are defeated decisively by Robert E. Lee's much smaller forces at the Battle of Chancellorsville, in Virginia.

MAY 10   The South suffers a huge blow as General Thomas "Stonewall" Jackson dies from wounds he received during the battle of Chancellorsville.

JUNE 3   Robert E. Lee launches his second invasion of the North; he heads into Pennsylvania with 75,000 Confederate troops.

JULY 1–3   The tide of war turns against the South as the Confederates are defeated at the Battle of Gettysburg in Pennsylvania.

JULY 4   Vicksburg, the last Confederate stronghold on the Mississippi River, surrenders to Ulysses S. Grant after a six-week siege.

JULY 13–16   Antidraft riots rip through New York City.

JULY 18   The black 54th Massachusetts Infantry Regiment under Colonel Robert Gould Shaw assaults a fortified Confederate position at Fort Wagner, South Carolina.

SEPTEMBER 19–20   A decisive Confederate victory takes place at Chickamauga, Tennessee.

NOVEMBER 19   President Lincoln delivers the Gettysburg Address.

NOVEMBER 23–25   Ulysses S. Grant's Union forces win an important victory at the Battle of Chattanooga, in Tennessee.

1864   **MARCH 9**   President Lincoln names Ulysses S. Grant general-in-chief of all the armies of the United States.

MAY 4   Ulysses S. Grant opens a massive, coordinated campaign against Robert E. Lee's Confederate armies in Virginia.

MAY 5–6 The Battle of the Wilderness is fought in Virginia.

MAY 8–12 The Battle of Spotsylvania is fought in Virginia.

JUNE 1–3 The Battle of Cold Harbor is fought in Virginia.

JUNE 15 Union forces miss an opportunity to capture Petersburg, Virginia; this results in a nine-month Union siege of the city.

SEPTEMBER 2 Atlanta, Georgia, is captured by Union forces led by William Tecumseh Sherman.

OCTOBER 19 Union general Philip H. Sheridan wins a decisive victory over Confederate general Jubal Early in the Shenandoah Valley of Virginia.

NOVEMBER 8 Abraham Lincoln is reelected president, defeating Democratic challenger George B. McClellan.

NOVEMBER 15 General William T. Sherman begins his March to the Sea from Atlanta.

DECEMBER 15–16 Confederate general John Bell Hood is defeated at Nashville, Tennessee, by Union forces under George H. Thomas.

DECEMBER 21 General Sherman reaches Savannah, Georgia; he leaves behind a path of destruction 300 miles long and 60 miles wide from Atlanta to the sea.

1865 Southern states begin to pass Black Codes.

JANUARY 31 The U.S. Congress approves the Thirteenth Amendment to the United States Constitution.

FEBRUARY 3 A peace conference takes place as President Lincoln meets with Confederate Vice President Alexander Stephens at Hampton Roads, Virginia; the meeting ends in failure, and the war continues.

MARCH 4 Lincoln delivers his second inaugural address ("With Malice Toward None"). Congress establishes the Freedmen's Bureau.

MARCH 25   Robert E. Lee's Army of Northern Virginia begins its last offensive with an attack on the center of Ulysses S. Grant's forces at Petersburg, Virginia. Four hours later, Lee's attack is broken.

APRIL 2   Grant's forces begin a general advance and break through Lee's lines at Petersburg. Lee evacuates Petersburg. Richmond, Virginia, the Confederate capital, is evacuated.

APRIL 9   Robert E. Lee surrenders his Confederate Army to Ulysses S. Grant at the village of Appomattox Court House, Virginia.

APRIL 14   John Wilkes Booth shoots President Lincoln at Ford's Theatre in Washington, D.C.

APRIL 15   President Abraham Lincoln dies. Vice President Andrew Johnson assumes the presidency.

APRIL 18   Confederate general Joseph E. Johnston surrenders to Union general William T. Sherman in North Carolina.

APRIL 26   John Wilkes Booth is shot and killed in a tobacco barn in Virginia.

DECEMBER   The Thirteenth Amendment is ratified.

1866   Congress approves the Fourteenth Amendment to the Constitution.

Congress passes the Civil Rights Act.

The responsibilities and powers of the Freedmen's Bureau are expanded by Congress. The legislation is vetoed by President Johnson, but Congress overrides his veto.

The Ku Klux Klan is established in Tennessee.

1867   Congress passes the Military Reconstruction Act.

Congress passes the Tenure of Office Act.

1868   The impeachment trial of President Andrew Johnson ends in acquittal.

Ulysses S. Grant is elected president.

1869   Congress approves the Fifteenth Amendment to the Constitution.

1871   The Ku Klux Klan Act is passed by Congress.

1872   President Grant is reelected.

1875   A new Civil Rights Act is passed.

1877   Rutherford B. Hayes assumes the presidency.

The Reconstruction Era ends.

Elizabeth Van Lew

It was a stormy April night when three men, riding in a mule-drawn wagon, approached the Oakwood Cemetery on the outskirts of Richmond, Virginia. The men were grateful for the rainy weather and the darkness, for it would give them cover during the task ahead. It was a task that would most likely result in their deaths if they were discovered.

The men got down from the wagon and moved slowly through the dark cemetery, looking for a particular spot. Finally, they found it: the careful marking, left by their informant, of a new grave.

The men—two brothers, Frederick and John Lohmann, and a bricklayer named Martin Lipscomb—had come to Oakwood Cemetery on the night of April 6, 1864, with a very grim task. They were to find the grave where Colonel Ulric Dahlgren had been secretly buried, dig up the body, and take it away.

Finding the marked spot, the men set to work with the help of an African-American gravedigger who was waiting for them in the cemetery. They pulled the simple pine box from the earth and opened it. Inside were the remains of Colonel Dahlgren. He was able to be identified by his right leg, which was missing below the knee. The men lifted the body from the box, carried it to the wagon, and covered it before reburying the now empty coffin. Then they somberly rode away with the body safely stowed in the wagon. A message was sent to the woman who had championed the effort to find Dahlgren's body. The petite Virginia aristocrat Elizabeth Van Lew was soon informed that her request had been carried out: Dahlgren's body had been removed from Oakwood Cemetery.

UNIONIST AND PATRIOT

Elizabeth Van Lew's interest in Dahlgren's body was not morbid curiosity but instead was inspired by compassion and respect. Colonel Dahlgren was an officer in the Union Army, fighting to preserve the United States in the Civil War. On March 1, 1864, Dahlgren had led a Federal division southward, clashing with Confederate forces on the outskirts of Richmond. Those Southerners in Richmond who supported the Confederacy and the secession of several Southern states (including Virginia) rushed to defend the capital. Richmond was both the capital of their state and of the Confederate States of America. Civilians who were unable to fight in the Confederate Army formed a local militia to defend the city. Through a series of military mistakes, Dahlgren and a small group of his men encountered the militia. Dahlgren was ambushed and killed.

Confederate newspapers soon published vivid accounts stating that Dahlgren's body had been found to be carrying papers that contained plans to burn Richmond once it was captured and to destroy Confederate President Jefferson Davis and his cabinet. A quick response from the Union Army command firmly stated that no such orders had been given. However, the propaganda inspired public outrage, especially in Richmond.

Elizabeth Van Lew's home (above) *was repeatedly searched for evidence of spy activity, but Confederate forces never uncovered proof of Van Lew's contributions to the Union cause. Known to Richmond citizens as "Crazy Bet," Van Lew created a large network of Union supporters that helped her gather and deliver information regarding the Confederates.*

Dahlgren was first buried where he was killed, in a shallow, muddy hole. But once his supposed plans were made public, the body was dug up and moved to a railroad station in Richmond, where crowds gathered to see it. They were undoubtedly pleased at the state of the corpse—the body had mockingly been dressed in a Confederate uniform, covered by a Confederate blanket. Dahlgren's wooden leg had been taken away, and the little finger of his left hand had been cut off. A small, thin man with red hair and a goatee, Dahlgren appeared to have died in agony.

Finally, after the crowds had jeered and ridiculed his body, Dahlgren was secretly taken away for burial. Jefferson Davis himself supposedly issued the order that no one was to reveal where the corpse had been buried.

Elizabeth Van Lew had read of all this in the Richmond papers and was horrified. Her religious beliefs suggested that all people should spend their final moments on Earth in a noble way, and that, after death, they should be surrounded and mourned by loved ones. She determined that Dahlgren's body should be found, removed, and after a period of mourning, be reburied on friendlier soil.

Van Lew, despite being a wealthy young member of the Richmond elite, was secretly a Unionist. From the moment that Virginia announced its secession from the United States in 1861, she felt betrayed. She considered herself a loyal American, and believed that Virginia—the birthplace of so many great presidents—had a special role in U.S. history and politics.

Van Lew's parents were not native Virginians. Her father, John Van Lew, had been born on Long Island in New York and moved to Richmond in the early 1800s to set up a hardware business. Her mother, Eliza, was born in Philadelphia, the daughter of a Patriot, Hilary Baker, who had participated in Pennsylvania's constitutional convention. Eliza Van Lew was a member of the Pennsylvania Abolition Society, one of the early and leading antislavery organizations in the United States. Eliza and John Van Lew met in Richmond, where Eliza's brother was living, and they were married at the very church where Patrick Henry had delivered his famous "Give me liberty or give me death" speech several decades earlier.

John Van Lew became a successful businessman, and he and his wife soon joined Richmond's elite society. They settled in an elegant three-story mansion, one of the finest in the city. The home soon not only housed the couple but also their daughter Elizabeth and two younger children, Anna and John, as well as several slaves.

Elizabeth was encouraged to read and study. In the early 1830s, she was sent to Philadelphia to live with family and attend the same school from which her mother had graduated. This exposure to life in Philadelphia no doubt contributed to her later sense of herself as not simply a Virginian, but as an American. Importantly, while in Philadelphia, she began to gain an understanding of the evils of slavery.

When Elizabeth was 25, John Van Lew died, leaving his wife and children with a considerable fortune. The terms of his will, however, prevented his wife from freeing the family's slaves outright. Instead, Eliza Van Lew began to allow her slaves to hire themselves out. This meant they could find their own employers and keep a percentage of what they earned so that, ultimately, they could move to a free state or purchase their own freedom.

UNDERCOVER ACTION

When the Civil War began, Elizabeth Van Lew knew that her own life and that of her family depended on her keeping her Union sympathies secret. Any man or woman suspected of supporting the Union could have his or her property seized and could be imprisoned.

Van Lew was inspired to take action when she learned of the horrible conditions in Richmond prisons for captured Union soldiers. She sent food, clothes, and other supplies to these soldiers, being careful to also periodically visit and bring supplies to Confederates as well. Soon, her connections with these Union soldiers led her to help shelter those who escaped from prison in a hidden room in the family home, ultimately helping them find their way to freedom.

From both Union and Confederate soldiers she learned details of Confederate troop positions and the numbers in the various divisions. She eventually built a connection with the commander of the Union troops, General Ulysses Grant, through her younger brother, who had escaped from Richmond

Colonel Ulric Dahlgren, son of a high-ranking naval officer, was already distinguished as a war hero before he participated in a raid on Richmond, Virginia. Knowing this, Confederate troops publicly displayed Dahlgren's body after he had been killed and buried it in a secret location. Elizabeth Van Lew and her contacts in the Richmond underground spy network located Dahlgren and gave him a proper burial.

and fled north when the Confederates wanted to draft him. Her brother had made his way to Grant's headquarters and urged him to make contact with his sister.

Van Lew had valuable information, and she also had valuable contacts—a knowledge of those who were Unionist sympathizers and an ability to draft them into a kind of spy network.

Miss Van Lew's Will

On September 30, 1900, the *New York Times* published an article detailing the contents of the will of Elizabeth Van Lew. The article makes clear that what was once a considerable fortune had dwindled away, spent largely in Van Lew's efforts to aid the Union during the Civil War:

> The will of Miss Elizabeth L. Van Lew, the old lady whose devotion to the cause of the Union during the war made her such a notable character, was offered for probate here [Richmond] today. All of the estate of the deceased is left to the two Misses Hall, nieces of the deceased.
>
> The most interesting feature of the will is a codicil in which Miss Van Lew leaves "to my dear friend, Mr. John Phillips Reynolds of Boston, all of my manuscript." This is believed to give a most interesting history of Miss Van Lew's eventful life and especially her signal services to the Union cause during the war. The will provides that all of the household furniture, which is of very old style, shall be sold in Boston. The old lady's idea for this was that her personal effects would bring a better price in the New England metropolis, where she had many sympathizers and was well known, than elsewhere.
>
> The estate is only valued at $5,000. The old homestead in which Miss Van Lew was born is included in the list. It was at one time one of the handsomest homes here, but is now much dilapidated.

Van Lew's own servants were included in this group. They were sent out to the family farm about a quarter of a mile (400 meters) outside Richmond, and there, carrying baskets of farm produce, they seldom attracted attention. But within those baskets were details of troop movements and other critical pieces of intelligence that would then be passed on to Union Army scouts. In some cases, baskets of eggs held a few hollowed-out eggs that contained hidden information for General Grant. In other cases the information would be hidden inside the soles of the servants' shoes. The network was soon so well established that Van Lew's team was sending information to Union commanders three times a week.

Van Lew spent most of her family fortune in an effort to help the Union cause. Informants could be expensive. It was costly to smuggle an escaped soldier from Richmond back to the safety of Northern territory. It was expensive—and dangerous—to pay an informant enough to persuade him to reveal the location of Colonel Dahlgren's body and then to smuggle his body from the cemetery and on to a safe and more honorable burial. But for Van Lew, honor and principle, and loyalty to her country, inspired her to take action. Her actions and outspokenness caused her and members of her family to come under suspicion. She was closely watched, but her wealth and social status—and the fact that she was a woman—made it difficult for even the most suspicious Confederate supporters to believe that "one of their own" might not be loyal to the Confederate cause.

A MORE FITTING FAREWELL

Elizabeth Van Lew and her mother joined a small circle of secret Unionists who gathered at the farm of William Rowley, a friend of Van Lew who owned land on the outskirts of Richmond. It was there that Colonel Dahlgren's body had been hidden after its removal from Oakwood Cemetery. They had come to pay their final respects to Dahlgren. This gathering was highly dangerous.

It might draw the attention of the authorities to the place where Dahlgren's body had been hidden, and if discovered, all those gathered there would certainly be imprisoned and possibly executed as traitors to the Confederate cause.

But Van Lew and the others felt that it was important for Dahlgren to be honored in death. Because his family could not be with him, they gathered as a kind of substitute family, to mourn him and surround him until he could be properly buried. They provided a metal coffin, more durable and noble than the flimsy pine box, and transferred his body gently into it. They cut off a lock of his hair as a keepsake that was secretly sent to Dahlgren's father. The coffin was sealed, then placed in Rowley's wagon and covered with several small peach trees.

Rowley then drove the wagon to the farm of another Unionist. On the way, he was stopped by a Confederate guard, but Rowley casually started a conversation with him about peach trees and how best to grow the delicate plants. The guard waved Rowley on, and Dahlgren's body was safely moved to the farm, some distance outside the city. It was on this farm that Dahlgren was buried. As Van Lew had wished, the grave was dug on friendly soil and Rowley planted a peach tree above it. As a final gesture, Van Lew ensured that a message was sent to Dahlgren's father telling him that his son's remains had been buried in a safe place, where "friends" would watch over him.

Van Lew continued her spying network until Richmond fell to the Union Army on April 3, 1865. When the extent of her work for the Union was discovered, Van Lew's reputation was destroyed in the eyes of her neighbors. No one socialized with her or her family, and she became an outcast in the city she loved.

But her work was so highly valued by General Ulysses Grant that, when he became president, he appointed Elizabeth Van Lew postmaster of Richmond in 1869. She became active in politics, a supporter of the Republican Party, an advocate for women's rights, and a frequent correspondent to Northern newspapers criticizing the treatment of African Americans in Richmond.

When her political career ended in the 1880s, she spent more and more time in her home, unwilling to face the hostility of her Richmond neighbors. She died on September 25, 1900, at the age of 83. The *New York Times* of October 25, 1900, described her as one whose "services to the Union cause made her notable," and explained that Northern friends would erect a monument over her grave, announcing to all what she had done for the Union cause.

North and
South Divided

A wide range of causes motivated those who chose to provide intelligence during the Civil War. Some believed passionately in the rights of the Southern states to secede from the United States. Others felt just as passionately that the union of states must be preserved. Some spied because they felt slavery was wrong, while others spied because they believed that states had the right to continue a practice so critical to the economic success of their region. Regardless of their motivations, most spies felt that what they were doing was the right thing to do.

This sense of obligation, and of honor, marked the Civil War. The spies were far from unusual in their desire to fight for what they believed to be right and just. More than 3 million Americans fought in the Civil War. More than 600,000 died in it.

There were large battles that marked the Civil War, in places such as Gettysburg, Shiloh, Manassas, and Antietam.

But armies also marched across farmland and through the streets of small towns, setting up their headquarters in homes and turning schools and churches into hospitals.

The war for many Americans was not something taking place in a distant land, something they read about only in the newspapers. It was happening in their own backyards. Their fathers, sons, brothers, and husbands were fighting—and dying—in it. It is for this reason that so many otherwise ordinary Americans became involved in spying during the Civil War. They did not need special training or skills. They listened and watched what was happening around them, and then they passed that information on to someone who needed it.

THE CAUSES

There were many factors that contributed to the outbreak of the Civil War. Economic issues played a key role in dividing the nation. In 1800, the population of the United States was nearly evenly split between North and South. By 1850, only a third of the nation's population lived in the South. Larger population numbers in the North brought a greater number of representatives for the Northern states in the U.S. Congress and greater political influence.

The nineteenth century also marked a change in lifestyle between the North and South. In the North, manufacturing became an important source of income. More people began to move to town and cities, and fewer were living on farms or employed in agriculture. Of the goods manufactured in the United States, 90 percent came from the North, bringing even greater wealth to that region.

As the South felt its political and economic influence begin to decline, fierce debates were fought on many political fronts. There were arguments about tariffs, or taxes on goods. There were arguments about admitting new states and territories into the United States. There were arguments about which legal rights belonged to the individual states and which belonged to the federal government. And there were arguments about slavery.

The issue of slavery's legality had been simmering since the time of the country's founding as an independent nation. It increasingly became a subject of national debate during the first half of the nineteenth century. The Mexican-American War (1846–1848) helped place the spotlight more firmly on what came to be called "the slavery question." After the war, significant areas of formerly Mexican territory had been added to the United States—territory that would eventually become the states of Arizona, New Mexico, Nevada, Utah, part of Colorado, and California. At one point the Midwest had been the focus of growth and development. Suddenly the focus was on the southwestern portion of the United States.

A debate arose in the Senate, one that was eventually echoed throughout the nation: whether or not slavery should be allowed in these new territories. Many Southerners, including Mississippi Senator Jefferson Davis, were outspoken in their belief that to prohibit slavery in these new territories would effectively prevent Southerners from settling in them. Davis's argument was that Southerners could not be prohibited from bringing their slaves into their new land to build farms and raise crops as they did in the South.

These divisions and arguments over states' rights ultimately led several of the Southern states to secede from the Union. The first was South Carolina, which seceded on December 20, 1860. Mississippi followed on January 9, 1861. A month later, Jefferson Davis received word that he had been unanimously elected president of the Confederate States of America, which numbered seven at the time that he assumed the office. In addition to Mississippi and South Carolina, the states of Alabama, Georgia, Florida, Texas, and Louisiana had voted to secede.

THE PENDING CONFLICT.

One of the main causes of the Civil War was the issue of states' rights, an argument that developed from the growing economic and cultural differences between the North and the South. Some Southern states believed that they should have the power to make decisions on issues regarding taxes and slavery. They came together and announced their independence, calling themselves the Confederate States of America or simply the Confederacy. Above, a political cartoon illustrates the growing conflict between the North and the South.

As Davis assumed the presidency of the Confederacy, Abraham Lincoln was being inaugurated as president of the United States. Both men would soon find themselves commanders-in-chief of opposing forces in a civil war.

THE WAR UNFOLDS

The first shots of the Civil War were fired at 4:30 A.M. on April 12, 1861, at Fort Sumter in Charleston, South Carolina. The fort had become the focal point for the unfolding conflict. South Carolina insisted that the fort was now its property and demanded that the 68 Union troops then occupying it evacuate the fort and turn it over to South Carolina authorities. The troops, acting under Lincoln's orders, refused.

On that early April morning, Confederate troops stationed outside the fort opened fire after weeks of waiting while supplies in the fort had steadily dwindled. The onslaught lasted a day and a half before Union troops finally surrendered. Citizens from Charleston gathered to cheer as the shots were fired. That first battle strengthened the determination of both the North and the South to fight for what they believed to be their own just cause.

President Lincoln issued a proclamation calling on the states to provide 75,000 militiamen for a 90-day term of service. Seven states had seceded before the shelling at Fort Sumter, and four more would soon follow: Virginia, Arkansas, Tennessee, and North Carolina. The U.S. Army at the time contained fewer than 17,000 men, and the majority of them were stationed in the far West.

In late May, the capital of the Confederacy was moved to Richmond, Virginia, from Montgomery, Alabama. A total of 11 states now formed the Confederacy. Its president, Jefferson Davis, responded to Lincoln's call for troops with the words that the Confederate states wanted peace "at any sacrifice, save that of honor and independence," but the South would "meet" the war being waged by Lincoln. As noted in Shelby Foote's *The Civil War: A Narrative*, Confederate Vice President Alexander H. Stephens was more defiant, stating: "Lincoln may bring his 75,000 troops against us. We fight for our homes, our fathers and mothers, our wives, brothers, sisters, sons and daughters! . . . We can call out a million of peoples if need be, and when they are cut down we can call another, and still another, until the last man of the South finds a bloody grave."

This was the language that marked the Civil War at its beginning. Ordinary Americans would soon be swept up in the conflict alongside soldiers, serving on the battlefield as nurses and attendants, and as spies.

"We Never Sleep"

When news of the coming war began to spread throughout the United States, there was no formal system for intelligence gathering in place. Today, there are intelligence-gathering divisions in government organizations such as the Central Intelligence Agency (CIA), the Federal Bureau of Investigation (FBI), and the National Security Agency (NSA), and within the branches of the military. The goal of these organizations is to protect the interests of the United States domestically and abroad. But, in the 1860s, there was no formal intelligence service attached to the military, and if there had been, its security might have been threatened.

It is important to remember that, at the time, there were no separate officer training programs for Northerners and Southerners. Instead, they were trained and served together, side by side. Indeed, Robert E. Lee, who would lead the Confederate Army, had first been offered the command of the Union Army.

But when his home state of Virginia seceded from the Union, Lee felt that his loyalty—and his military experience—must be given in service to his home state.

For this reason, when war seemed increasingly likely, there was a great sense of uncertainty about who could be trusted. Intelligence-gathering efforts at the beginning were carried out in secret. Once sides had been chosen and those in the military with Southern sympathies had left to serve in the Confederate Army, the process of intelligence gathering could be carried out with slightly more certainty.

Before the war broke out, concerns centered around protecting the nation's capital and ensuring that its newly elected president, Abraham Lincoln, could safely be inaugurated. Washington, D.C., was considered by many to be a Southern city. Its mayor and chief of police both supported the secession movement, and a part-time general from Virginia headed its militia. Perhaps more worrisome, the majority of the nation's troops were stationed in the West. In January 1861, a small division—little more than 300 Marines—was all that was protecting the capital from a military strike from the South. There was great concern that an attack on the capital would take place in order to block president-elect Lincoln from taking office.

A small team of detectives was hired to protect Lincoln as he traveled to Washington by train. They uncovered evidence of a plot to assassinate him when he passed through Baltimore, just before arriving for his inauguration, and they persuaded Lincoln to change his travel plans. Instead of a fancy reception in Baltimore, Lincoln quickly passed through the city in the middle of the night, arriving secretly in Washington well ahead of schedule and without any formal ceremony. Southerners would later jump on this secretive beginning to Lincoln's presidency as evidence of his cowardice.

Accompanying Lincoln on the train trip was Allan Pinkerton, the head of a Chicago-based detective agency. Pinkerton would become one of the most famous spies of the Civil War, and would form the war's first "secret service" organization.

ALLAN PINKERTON

Pinkerton was born in Glasgow, Scotland, on August 25, 1819. His father, William Pinkerton, was a police sergeant who was killed in a political riot when Allan was still a young boy. Allan had never been a strong student, and after his father's death he left school altogether, going to work to help support himself and his mother. Pinkerton worked first for a pattern maker and then as an apprentice to McCauley Cooperage Works, where he learned the craft of barrel making. This was a valuable skill at a time when nearly all goods—food, clothing, tools, and more— were shipped in barrels. Pinkerton had a talent for this work and became one of the company's most skilled craftsmen.

At the time, there was a movement sweeping Scotland calling for greater representation in the British government. Pinkerton joined one of these groups—the Charters—but the British government was not at all open to any hint of revolution or rebellion. Those suspected of involvement in the Charters were hunted down. The outspoken, 22-year-old Pinkerton was quickly identified as one of the Charters' members, and orders were issued for his arrest.

Pinkerton had been promoted to supervisor at McCauley Cooperage Works. On March 13, 1842, he was due to marry a young woman from Edinburgh, Joan Carfrae. One of his friends rushed in just as the wedding ceremony was ending and warned Pinkerton that soldiers were approaching to arrest him. Pinkerton and his new bride quickly slipped away. They hid until the following morning, when they made their way to the docks and boarded a boat bound for Canada.

As the ship neared Canada it encountered a fierce storm that drove it some 200 miles (320 kilometers) from its intended destination of Halifax. The ship finally rammed into a rocky

By the time President Abraham Lincoln (center) took office, seven states had seceded from the Union. After the first shots were fired at Fort Sumter, the conflict escalated into a full-out war between the North and the South. Although Lincoln did not oppose slavery when he was elected to the presidency, his opinion gradually shifted and his carefully worded Emancipation Proclamation helped bring about the end of slavery in the United States.

reef near the coast of Nova Scotia and began to sink. Pinkerton and his wife lost all of their possessions and were forced into the chilly water along with the other surviving passengers. They were able to make their way to the beach, where they were finally rescued by another ship.

Pinkerton had originally planned to make his home in Quebec but the stressful arrival in Canada convinced him to try his luck farther south, in the United States. He had heard some of his fellow passengers discussing a new settlement in the United States that was rapidly growing into a major city: Chicago. Goods were flowing in and out of Chicago as it grew, and Pinkerton sensed that there was an opportunity there for a skilled barrel maker in a new city that needed craftsmen.

Pinkerton and his wife made their way to Chicago, staying in barns because they had no money to pay for an inn or boarding house. The city, in its earliest years, was a rough and rather inhospitable place. The streets were deeply rutted, not paved. Buildings had been put up so quickly that the storefronts were often made of mismatched lumber. Pinkerton met a group of Scotsmen shortly after his arrival, and from them he learned of a local firm, Lill's Brewery, that was hiring barrel makers, and he went to work.

Pinkerton earned enough money to set up his own barrel shop in Dundee, some 40 miles (65 km) from Chicago. Dundee was a farming region where many Scottish immigrants had settled. The farmers there had been paying high prices to buy barrels made in Chicago, transport them to Dundee, fill them with farming goods, and then transport them back to Chicago. Pinkerton set up a small shop on the banks of the Fox River, which flowed toward Chicago, and called his new business Pinkerton's One and Original Cooperage of Dundee.

Pinkerton's prices were far lower than those for barrels made in Chicago, and his business quickly grew from a one-man workshop to a large plant that employed 10 barrel makers.

Allan Pinkerton (sitting right), a Scottish immigrant, left barrel making to become a detective after solving two major cases in the Midwest. As Pinkerton's reputation for sleuthing grew, he developed a friendship with Union general George McClellan. McClellan asked Pinkerton to provide military intelligence for him during the war.

As his business was growing, so was his family. He became the father of a son and twins—a girl and a boy.

One day, Pinkerton went looking for less expensive materials to use to make barrel hoops. He was exploring a nearby island in the Fox River when he happened upon a path leading deeper into a cluster of trees. He followed the path and discovered a campsite that seemed to have been recently used.

A band of counterfeiters had been spreading fake money throughout northern Illinois, and local lawmen had suspected that they might be hiding some of the counterfeit money in Dundee. They so far had been unable to find the counterfeiters and break the ring. Pinkerton suspected that the hidden campsite might be connected to the counterfeiters, and he shared his suspicions with the local sheriff.

For several days, Pinkerton and the sheriff staked out the island, hiding in the trees and waiting. On the fifth day, their wait was rewarded. A flash of torchlight, a low sound, and then a group of men appeared on the path. They were covered in dirt and carrying spades, shovels, and bulging flour sacks.

Pinkerton and the sheriff boldly jumped out from the trees, pointing shotguns at the men. They arrested them, and when word of Pinkerton's efforts became known, he was asked by members of the town council to help uncover who was serving as leader of the local branch of the counterfeit ring. A landowner was suspected. Pinkerton was asked to watch and follow the man and, if possible, offer to buy some of the suspect bills.

Pinkerton successfully uncovered the local man's involvement and then took the investigation one step further. He determined to follow the chain to Chicago and uncover its Midwest headquarters. Working with Chicago law enforcement, he set up a trap that enabled the arrest of many members of the counterfeit ring.

The Cook County sheriff in Chicago was so impressed by Pinkerton's efforts that he offered the Scotsman a full-time job as an investigator. Pinkerton had loved the excitement of the investigation and the satisfaction of feeling that he had helped bring an end to a crime wave. He accepted the offer and moved his family to Chicago. It was 1848, and Pinkerton would quickly become noted for his impressive arrest record and for his skills in investigating burglaries and murders. By 1850, Pinkerton had decided to open his own detective agency.

PRIVATE EYE

In the years following Pinkerton's arrival in the United States, Chicago quickly grew into a major city. It was a transportation hub in the country, and a gateway to the booming western territories. As a police detective there, Pinkerton solved some theft cases involving the Rock Island and Illinois Central Railroad, one of the major railroad companies headquartered in the Midwest. When he decided to set up his own agency, Pinkerton approached the rail company's president, George B. McClellan, to offer the services of the new firm. It was a smart connection. McClellan was a military officer who, as civil war threatened, would be the U.S. Army's ranking major general helping to oversee the protection of the nation's capital.

Pinkerton was skilled not only at solving cases but also at promoting his agency's ability to solve cases. Pinkerton's National Detective Agency was the frequent subject of glowing newspaper articles as the agency solved crimes and captured thieves and murderers. Pinkerton helped create a logo to publicize his agency. The logo featured an eye with the motto "We Never Sleep" underneath it. Pinkerton himself was often referred to as "The Eye," which eventually brought about the term *private eye*.

Pinkerton was careful about who he would hire to serve as a detective in his agency, and he insisted on strict codes of behavior for his staff. Pinkerton detectives were not allowed to drink, play cards, smoke, or use slang. The firm gained a reputation for efficiency and honesty. Pinkerton even hired the country's first female detective, Kate Warne, who persuaded Pinkerton that a woman would be able to befriend the wives and girlfriends of suspects and gain information through them.

Warne successfully proved her skills at obtaining information and observing details that proved valuable. She convinced Pinkerton to hire additional female agents, some 40 years before women were allowed to join local police forces.

By 1861, there was great unrest spreading throughout the country, as war seemed likely. There was particular concern that sabotage might target railroads even before war broke out. By the time this was going on, the Pinkerton firm had already gained a national reputation. The Philadelphia, Wilmington and Baltimore Railroad hired Pinkerton to protect its line, a major network along the East Coast. Pinkerton placed several agents at critical posts along the rail line. He stationed himself in Baltimore, but neither he nor his agents could uncover any plot to disrupt the railroad.

What they did uncover, instead, was evidence of a plot to assassinate Abraham Lincoln as he traveled by train to his inauguration. One of Pinkerton's agents, Timothy Webster, befriended members of a secessionist group called the Knights of the Golden Circle and learned that several assassins had already been selected to kill Lincoln when he passed through Baltimore on February 23, 1861. The president-elect's schedule had been printed in the newspaper, so the plotters knew exactly what time he would arrive in the city.

Pinkerton knew that he needed to contact Lincoln immediately to alert him to the danger. Pinkerton knew one of the members of Lincoln's Illinois staff. He also knew that Lincoln was scheduled to arrive in Philadelphia in a few hours' time for a parade. Pinkerton quickly took a train to Philadelphia, found the staff member, and was soon ushered into a meeting with Lincoln himself.

Pinkerton explained to Lincoln what Webster had learned and also expressed his fear that Baltimore police officials might be part of the conspiracy. He convinced Lincoln to fake an illness and then slip out into a carriage. Pinkerton threw a scarf over the president-elect, and he and another agent smuggled him onto a small passenger train. As the train pulled out of the depot, one of Pinkerton's agents climbed a nearby telegraph pole and cut the line to prevent anyone who might have followed them from wiring ahead to the conspirators in Baltimore.

Kate Warne and several other Pinkerton agents, all heavily armed, were on the train. Agents had been stationed at many of the bridges and crossings along the route, charged with signaling by light that all was well and their plan had not been uncovered. Pinkerton himself stood on the train's rear platform, staring out into the night and watching for the signals.

The train pulled into Baltimore at 3:30 A.M. More Pinkerton agents met them there, forming a barrier around the president-elect as he was transferred from one small train to another. The connecting train was carefully checked before Lincoln was allowed to board, and it then moved on the remaining miles to Washington, arriving just after 6 A.M. Little fanfare greeted the man who would become the nation's sixteenth president. Confederate newspapers learned of this effort to protect Lincoln from assassination and ridiculed the image of the tall president-elect, covered in a scarf, creeping into the capital to assume the presidency.

Pinkerton did not wait to see the president inaugurated. Instead, he returned to Chicago. Before long, he would again find himself working for Lincoln.

SECRET SERVICE

Shortly after his inauguration, with war on the horizon, Lincoln summoned a friend from Illinois, a Mexican-American War hero and president of the Illinois Central Railroad, George McClellan. Lincoln asked McClellan to head the Army of the Potomac, charged with guarding Washington from attack. McClellan brought Pinkerton with him, knowing the value of the Scotsman's detective work and knowing, too, that intelligence gathering would be vital in protecting the capital.

Pinkerton later claimed that he was asked by Lincoln to form a secret police, or "secret service," that would officially lead the government's efforts in intelligence gathering. But when Lincoln discussed the nomination with his cabinet, he faced resistance. The commander of the U.S. Army, General Winfield Scott, had another candidate in mind to head up the secret service—a former lawyer from Ohio named Lafayette Baker. As Lincoln pushed for Pinkerton and the cabinet debated, Pinkerton grew impatient. McClellan had asked Pinkerton to work directly for him, providing military intelligence and assisting him in questioning men who were captured. Pinkerton agreed.

At the age of 42, Pinkerton left his business and became a secret agent, traveling through Kentucky, Tennessee, and Mississippi to watch and report on Confederate military preparations. Much of what he did in those years was undercover. His reports did not reveal where he was stationed. He used the name "E.J. Allen" as an alias and refused to tell anyone exactly who was working for him. Instead, he used only initials when he was submitting vouchers to the Department of War for their pay. There were some 28 agents working for Pinkerton during the 16 months he provided military intelligence to McClellan.

The organization set up by Pinkerton and McClellan became an innovation in military intelligence. This was mainly because of its formal, independent structure. In the nation's previous wars, specifically the Revolutionary and Mexican-American wars, intelligence was not conducted by a specific organization within the military. Pinkerton's orders were to focus on espionage (gathering information about the Confederate Army) and interrogation of prisoners, deserters, and refugees. This was a specific and limited portion of the intelligence used during the war. Pinkerton's agents would linger in towns where military camps had been established, learning details of troops

After uncovering information regarding a plot to assassinate Abraham Lincoln, private detective Allan Pinkerton rushed to Baltimore and helped smuggle the president into Washington, D.C. An impressed Lincoln asked Pinkerton to form a secret service agency, one that would infiltrate Southern ranks in order to obtain enemy information. Pinkerton's organization was so successful, it served as the model for the FBI. Above, an illustration depicts Lincoln's secret arrival in Washington, D.C., with Pinkerton closely following the president.

movements, who was in command, where fortifications had been placed, and the strength of the artillery.

As the war began, much of Pinkerton's efforts focused on Richmond, the capital of the Confederacy. It was far easier for spies to move unnoticed through a city than a military camp. Disguised as messengers or smugglers, the agents would pass

Greenhow's Intelligence Reports

Among Allan Pinkerton's successes during the Civil War was the uncovering of Washington hostess Rose Greenhow as a spy for the Confederacy. Pinkerton arrested Greenhow on August 23, 1861, after papers found in her home revealed that she was supplying information to Confederate contacts. The papers included the following reports, reprinted in Edwin C. Fishel's *The Secret War for the Union*:

31 [July]
All is activity. McClellan is busy night and day but the panick is great and the attack is hourly expected. They believe that the attack will be made simultaneous from Edwards Ferry and Baltimore. Every effort is being made to find out who gave the alarm. A troop of cavalry will start from here this morning to Harpers Ferry. Don't give time for reorganizing.

[About Aug. 5]
There are 45.000 on Va. Side 15.000 around this City to wit Up the river above Chain Bridge[,] at Tennallytown[,] Bladensburg— across Anacostia Branch & commanding every approach to the City. If McClellan's [sic] can be permitted to prepare he expects to surprise you but now [he] is preparing against one. Look out for mas[ked] batteries wherever you go. Their reliance this time is on abundance of artillery—which they have disposed formidably.

through town, claiming to be able to transport goods or information to secessionist sympathizers in the North.

Pinkerton eventually moved the base of his operation to Washington, with a goal of exposing the Confederate sympathizers in the capital. Valuable information was leaking out of the city, and Pinkerton soon uncovered a major source: a popular,

At proper time an effort will be made here to cut their telegraph wires and if possible to spike their guns wherever they are left unmanned. A line of daily communication is now open through Alexandria. Send couriers [three words unreadable] facilities enroute & where these dispatches enter yr lines below Alex [three or four words unreadable] we will endeavor [word or words unreadable] you.

[no date]
On the 16th an order was given at War Department for the purchase of 80 [one word undecipherable]. A military road is opened from Tenleytown round by Blairs to Bladensburg. Strong works with heavy guns, but they forget the fortifications of Paris. Some sixteenth [five words unreadable] they cant raise them. I am watching the Habeas Corpus Case as they will lose largely by it. Only 50 millions of the loan is available. The plan is now masterly inactivity. I will in a day or so send drawings of the Northern defences of the city. You give me no instructions and not being a military man I can only trust to my untutored judgment as to what is of value. All that I sent is reliable. All efforts are being made to raise an army. Peter [?Jornan] near Laurel Md. General Hiram Walbridge are spies. One regiment with ambulances passed over Long Bridge Saturday night and Battery to-day. Great deal of ordnance stores, some heavy pieces. This goes by safe hands but do not talk with any one about news from here as the birds of the air bring back. But I wish I could see you as I know much that a letter cannot give. Give me some instructions. You know that my soul is in the cause and that I would venture much. . . .

connected, and wealthy widow named Rose Greenhow who had counted former president James Buchanan and members of Lincoln's cabinet as guests at her home on numerous occasions. Pinkerton's agents uncovered evidence that Greenhow was providing information to the Confederacy, and it was Pinkerton himself who arrested Greenhow on August 23, 1861.

Greenhow was held under house arrest. She was joined by other women who were believed to have passed on information to the Confederacy. The home was soon known as Fort Greenhow. Eventually, Greenhow was ordered to be sent to Richmond. The Department of War accidentally ordered her release earlier than had been planned and she arrived in Richmond while several of Pinkerton's agents were still doing undercover work there. Greenhow's group knew Pinkerton's people by sight. The agents were spotted, quickly captured, and hanged.

END OF SERVICE

Critics have charged that because Pinkerton overestimated Confederate numbers, General McClellan was led to be more cautious. And McClellan's cautiousness led to military failures that extended the war. More recent reports have revealed that Pinkerton's numbers were, in fact, made after instructions from McClellan to err on the side of caution to avoid surprise from enemy forces that had not been counted. Pinkerton's efforts also relied on questioning captured prisoners, many of whom provided information that was more rumor than fact.

Pinkerton's alias of "E.J. Allen" was blown in December 1861, when he took it upon himself to investigate the condition of African Americans in the Washington city jail. There was no specific military reason for his investigation, but he quickly released what he had learned to the U.S. Senate. The information was sympathetic to the African Americans and prompted a backlash from a Washington newspaper, the *Star*. The *Star* claimed that Washington had been flooded with African Americans since the war began, and that if they were given jobs, there would not be enough jobs for white men. The paper also revealed that "E.J. Allen" was simply an alias for Pinkerton, and it referred to Pinkerton's agents as a "gang" intent on supplying information for abolitionists to use to stir up trouble.

McClellan's army suffered several critical defeats and Lincoln finally replaced McClellan as commander of the Army of the Potomac. The new commander, Major General Ambrose Burnside, did not wish to use Pinkerton's intelligence service. Pinkerton's old nemesis, Lafayette Baker, was soon appointed the Department of War's chief detective.

For the remaining years of the war, Pinkerton's government work involved investigating cases of fraud and civil crimes. He left Washington in 1862 and, after the war ended, returned to Chicago and resumed the operation of his detective agency. Pinkerton's sons soon joined the agency and helped in the effort to track notorious outlaws such as Jesse James and Butch Cassidy.

Pinkerton died on July 1, 1884. His agency continued to thrive long after his death, as did his reputation as one of the most famous spies of the Civil War. His successes would be followed by more sophisticated efforts to recruit local citizens as spies rather than relying on the efforts of trained agents. Still, the information he provided was critical in the early years of the war, and his techniques would later provide a model for the FBI.

Rose O'Neal Greenhow

One of the most celebrated accomplishments of Allan Pinkerton and his agents during his time as a Civil War spy was the uncovering of the spying operation run by a wealthy Washington widow, Rose O'Neal Greenhow. Confederate leaders credited Greenhow's information with providing critical assistance, making possible a Confederate victory in the First Battle of Manassas (also known as Bull Run).

Greenhow was born in Montgomery County, Maryland, in 1817. Nicknamed "Wild Rose," as a girl she received one of the finest educations available to young ladies at that time. She spent considerable time in nearby Washington, and her marriage to Robert Greenhow, an intellectual Virginian who served in the State Department, brought her to the capital city to establish a home that became the center of many of the city's finest parties and most celebrated gatherings.

Greenhow enjoyed exceptional ties to many of the leading politicians of the time. She was an aunt of Mrs. Stephen

Douglas, the wife of the Illinois senator who had gained notoriety for openly supporting the rights of new territories such as Kansas and Nebraska to choose whether or not to allow slavery. Senator Douglas later unsuccessfully challenged Abraham Lincoln for the presidency in 1860. Greenhow was also related by marriage to former president James Madison and his wife, Dolley, and was a close friend of former U.S. President James Buchanan. Even Allan Pinkerton was forced to describe her as a "very remarkable woman" whose abilities and contacts had given her "an almost superhuman power."

In the course of his work for the state department, Robert Greenhow moved his family to Mexico City in 1850, and later to San Francisco, where he was fatally injured in 1854. Rose Greenhow then returned with her four daughters to Washington, where she skillfully developed friendships with both Northerners and Southerners as the nation teetered toward civil war.

Because of her connection to Stephen Douglas, it is perhaps not surprising that Greenhow was unfriendly to Abraham Lincoln when he arrived in Washington in 1861 to assume the presidency. She was a strong supporter of the rights of Southern states to secede from the Union. As the country divided she determined to use her connections to provide valuable information to the Southern cause.

One of the first steps was to set up a route for her information. She chose Thomas Jordan, a Virginian she knew who had been serving in the U.S. Army until Virginia seceded. Jordan resigned his commission and prepared to join the Confederate forces, but first he and Greenhow set up a system of communication, creating a simple code that could be used for any information Greenhow might pass to the South.

Jordan served directly under General Pierre G.T. Beauregard, who had been one of the Confederate heroes at Fort Sumter and then was given command at Manassas, a short distance from Washington. Greenhow learned through her contacts of

Rose Greenhow, widow and socialite, was one of the Confederacy's most celebrated spies. Charming and popular, Greenhow invited members of Washington, D.C.'s elite to her house, where they divulged important military information. Armed with this knowledge, Greenhow routinely sent coded messages through Confederate supporters to officials in the South. Investigator Allan Pinkerton exposed Greenhow's activities and had her arrested and imprisoned with her daughter, Rose (above).

a planned Union Army advance across the Potomac River and sent a message warning of it to Beauregard. The messenger was a lovely young woman named Bettie Duval, who carried the warning sewn up in a piece of black silk, which she then used to tie up her long black hair. The warning inspired Beauregard to immediately make plans for the coming attack.

A second message, this time sent by a male messenger some seven days later, contained further information. It reported to Beauregard on the four routes upon which the troops were marching, as well as a greatly exaggerated count of the troops. (Greenhow reported some 55,000, whereas the actual number was probably closer to 35,000.) Scouts whom Beauregard sent out confirmed many of the details, and the general was able to immediately reposition some of his troops to prepare for the attack.

The Battle of Manassas (also called the Battle of Bull Run) would be the first major land battle of the Civil War. Both sides were confident that this might be the battle that would decide the outcome of what they were sure would be a swift war. But the smoke, noise, and violence were overwhelming to many who had expected a glorious victory, and the outcome proved far different from what they had expected. By the end of that day—July 21, 1861—some 900 men lay dead in a battle that would merely mark the beginning of a long and bloody war. The Union forces retreated to Washington, and the Confederate forces could claim victory.

SECRET INFORMATION

Greenhow hoped that the Confederate forces would follow up the success at Manassas with an attack on Washington. She made plans with a network of Southern sympathizers to cut telegraph wires when such an attack occurred. She also asked her contact, Jordan, for instructions as to what information would prove most helpful.

Greenhow built a close friendship—some have suggested a romantic relationship—with Henry Wilson, a Republican senator from Massachusetts. Wilson would later serve as vice president of the United States under Ulysses Grant from 1873 to 1875. At the time of his friendship with Greenhow he was best known as a strong opponent of slavery. Particularly valuable from Greenhow's point of view was Wilson's role as chairman of the Senate's Military Affairs Committee, where he had access to, among other figures, the number of heavy guns and other artillery in the Washington defenses. He shared these figures with Greenhow, who quickly reported them to her Confederate contact.

In addition to obtaining information from Wilson and other friends in high places, Greenhow also used a network of informants who walked around Washington where the troops were gathering. These informants put together information based on the troop movements, on where fortifications were being built, and on rumors they heard on the street. The bulk of Greenhow's information focused on what was happening in Washington and on what could fairly easily be observed.

It was Greenhow's prominence in Washington society that would eventually prove her undoing. She was well known as being sympathetic to the secessionist cause. Many of the visitors to her home were known to be secessionists. Washington military officials recognized that the Confederates stationed at Manassas had not been surprised by the North's attack, and suspected that someone in Washington had tipped them off.

Allan Pinkerton was hired to help in the mission to safeguard Washington against Confederate attack and was specifically directed to keep an eye on Rose Greenhow as a possible spy. Because she had friends in government and friends who supported secession, she was an obvious suspect.

Greenhow's home was watched for nearly a month. Then one August night, Pinkerton was performing the surveillance

Believing the Civil War would be a short-lived conflict, Senator Henry Wilson anticipated a Union win at Manassas, Virginia, and even brought sandwiches for the troops. The South, however, defeated Federal troops at the Battle of Manassas and rumors of Wilson's relationship with Rose Greenhow, a suspected Confederate spy, sullied his reputation. It was later revealed that Wilson, along with other high-ranking officials, had relayed important military information to Greenhow.

himself when he noticed a Union Army officer leaving the home. Pinkerton and one of his men followed the officer, who then began to run. They followed him back to his quarters, where he turned around and placed them under military arrest. He left them with a guard and disappeared for some 20 minutes—enough time to dispose of any incriminating papers he might have been carrying. Pinkerton and his agent spent the night under guard before being released the following morning. Pinkerton quickly made his way back to Greenhow's home.

The house was searched, and Pinkerton and his men discovered a wealth of incriminating papers, including copies of the

"Letter from a Southern Lady in Prison"

On November 17, 1861, Rose Greenhow wrote a letter to Secretary of State William Seward, complaining of her treatment while under house arrest. A copy of the letter was sent to Richmond and published by the Richmond *Whig*, leading to Greenhow's imprisonment. The letter is part of the collection of Rose Greenhow's papers maintained at Duke University:

> Sir—For nearly three months I have been confined, a close prisoner, shut out from air and exercise, and denied all communication with family and friends.
>
> "Patience is said to be a great virtue," and I have practised it to my utmost capacity of endurance. . . .
>
> In the careful analysis of my papers I deny the existence of a line I had not a perfect right to have written, or to have received. Freedom of speech and of opinion is the birthright of Americans, guaranteed to us by our Charter of Liberty, the Constitution of the United States. I have exercised my prerogative [right], and have openly avowed my sentiments. During the political struggle, I opposed your Republican party with every instinct of self-preservation. I believed your success a virtual nullification of the Constitution, and that it would entail upon us the direful consequences which have ensued. These sentiments have doubtless been found recorded among my papers, and I hold them as rather a proud record of my sagacity [wisdom].
>
> I must be permitted to quote from a letter of yours, in regard to Russell of the London Times, which you conclude with these admi-

reports Greenhow had sent to Jordan. Some had been placed in her stove, where she undoubtedly intended to destroy them at some point. Some were torn up and had to be reassembled. All were in code, but Greenhow had also kept the original, decoded version of one of the documents, which Pinkerton could then use to decode the other documents.

rable words: "Individual errors of opinion may be tolerated, as long as good sense is left to combat them." By way of illustrating theory and practice, here am I, a prisoner in sight of the Executive Mansion, in sight of the Capitol where the proud statesmen of our land have sung their paeans to the blessings of our free institutions. Comment is idle. Freedom of thought, every right pertaining to the citizen has been suspended by what, I suppose, the President calls a "military necessity." A blow has been struck, by this total disregard of all civil rights, against the present system of Government, far greater in its effects than the severance of the Southern States. . . .

My object is to call your attention to the fact: that during this long imprisonment, I am yet ignorant of the causes of my arrest; that my house has been seized and converted into a prison by the Government; that the valuable furniture it contained has been abused and destroyed; that during some periods of my imprisonment I have suffered greatly for want of proper and sufficient food. . . .

The "iron heel of power" may keep down, but it cannot crush out, the spirit of resistance in a people armed for the defence of their rights; and I tell you now, sir, that you are standing over a crater, whose smothered fires in a moment may burst forth.

It is your boast, that thirty-three bristling fortifications now surround Washington. The fortifications of Paris did not protect Louis Phillippe [the king of France, forced to step down by the Revolution of 1848] when his hour had come.

In conclusion, I respectfully ask your attention to this protest, and have the honor to be, &c., (Signed)

Rose O. N. Greenhow

In all, detectives found eight intelligence reports in Greenhow's home dating from July 31 to August 21, 1861. Rose Greenhow and her eight-year-old daughter, Rose, were placed under house arrest.

Within a week, other women suspected of being Confederate informants were brought to Greenhow's home to be held, earning the house the nickname "Fort Greenhow." Greenhow was not allowed access to newspapers, her mail was censored, and for the first week, guards watched her night and day. At first only her sister and niece were allowed to visit her, but gradually these rules were relaxed slightly by Pinkerton, undoubtedly to see who else might visit her. Pinkerton's plan was to follow these visitors and see if Greenhow was continuing to smuggle out information.

She was. Several warnings of upcoming Federal attacks (which proved false) were carried to Confederate officials during this time, and at least one of them is definitely known to have come from Greenhow. Jordan suspected that Pinkerton was aware of her efforts and warned his Confederate superiors that the information her messages contained could no longer be trusted.

The forced confinement weighed heavily on Greenhow, and finally she wrote a letter to Lincoln's secretary of state, William Seward, another of her important friends, complaining of her treatment. A copy of the letter made its way into the newspaper in Richmond, the capital of the Confederacy, and then was reprinted in the North. In the North, outraged readers complained that a woman who, after all, was guilty of treason should not be able to freely send correspondence (or copies of correspondence) to Richmond. Greenhow and her eight-year-old daughter were then sent to Washington's Old Capitol Prison.

Greenhow was held in prison for several months before a decision was reached to send her to Richmond. There she was welcomed as a heroine. The president of the Confederacy, Jefferson Davis, praised her for her role in the successful outcome at Manassas. Greenhow later described this moment as the proudest of her whole life.

CONFEDERATE HEROINE

Famous for her spying and celebrated as a heroine of the Confederate cause, Greenhow became a valuable public relations symbol, traveling throughout the Confederacy for nearly a year. By August 1863, the Confederate states hoped to gain support and official recognition from England and France, and Greenhow was sent overseas to help publicize the Confederate cause.

To make the journey, Greenhow and her daughter took a blockade runner to Bermuda, where they transferred to a British ship. Many historians suggest that she carried official papers from Jefferson Davis to Europe, and it is certain that she met with many members of Europe's nobility. In Paris she met with Emperor Napoleon III and later enrolled her daughter in a French convent school. In England, she was received at the court of Queen Victoria and met with several British leaders. While in England, Greenhow's memoir, *My Imprisonment and the First Year of Abolition Rule at Washington*, was published in London and received some favorable press.

After a year abroad, Greenhow boarded a British blockade runner in 1864 and prepared for the journey home. She was carrying with her official papers and a considerable amount of British gold.

As the ship approached Wilmington, North Carolina, it was spotted by a Union patrol and chased as it neared the mouth of the Cape Fear River. Greenhow and five others jumped into a rowboat and attempted to escape to shore, but the rowboat capsized. The five who were with her survived, but Greenhow drowned. Some reports suggested that she was weighted down by the British gold she was carrying in a money belt.

When her body was recovered and brought to Wilmington, a large crowd of women lined the wharf to meet it. She was buried with full military honors, her coffin wrapped in the Confederate flag and carried by Confederate troops. The marker for her grave states simply: "Mrs Rose O'N. Greenhow, a bearer of dispatchs [sic] to the Confederate Government."

Belle Boyd

Many of the women who would become spies during the Civil War began their service volunteering to help the wounded in the many makeshift hospitals set up throughout the North and South. One of the most famous of these was a young Confederate spy named Belle Boyd, who recounted her adventures in the autobiographical *Belle Boyd in Camp and Prison*.

Boyd was born in 1844 in Martinsburg in the Shenandoah Valley, an area that was then part of Virginia but today is in West Virginia. The Boyds had prominent relatives in many parts of the South, including New Orleans and Kentucky. They were also distantly related to George Randolph, who would serve as the Confederate secretary of war. But Belle's family was less well off than many of her relatives.

She spent her early childhood as a tomboy in the rural countryside, climbing trees and riding wildly around the area on horseback. Her family wanted her to have a proper education, and at age 12 she was sent to the Mount Washington Female

College in Baltimore. After four years she returned home and her family made arrangements for her to have her debut into Washington society. In her memoir, Boyd described this time in late 1860 in Washington as "brilliant":

> The Senate and Congress halls were nightly dignified by the presence of our ablest orators and statesmen; the salons of the wealthy and the talented were filled to overflowing; the theatres were crowded to excess, and for the last time for many years to come the daughters of the North and the South commingled in sisterly love and friendship.

Boyd was frequently a guest at the home of John Floyd, secretary of war under then-president James Buchanan. Floyd resigned to join the Confederate Army, and there was talk of secession at his home. When Fort Sumter fell and Virginia seceded, Belle Boyd returned to her home as a teenager who had become a fierce supporter of the Confederate cause.

At home, Boyd discovered that her 44-year-old father had enlisted in the Confederate Army. She and some of her friends soon organized a trip to visit the troops, where the lively and flirtatious Boyd found more excitement. In those early days of the war, the troops had not yet encountered the grim reality of battle. Boyd described the scene as "joyous" and declared, "A true woman always loves a real soldier."

Boyd had volunteered at the local hospital and was helping to care for the soldiers there when Federal troops began entering local homes. Boyd claimed to have shot one of the Federal soldiers who, despite her mother's protests, had attempted to raise a Union flag over her home and then threatened the two women. After the mortally wounded soldier was carried off, his commander returned to investigate the incident. Boyd used her charm, describing the victim as "mad drunk"· and saying his language was "as offensive as it is possible to conceive." She was successful enough not only to avoid further punishment but instead to have Union Army guards posted at her home for protection. A representative checked each day to make sure that there were no further problems.

This was the beginning of Boyd's contacts with the Union Army. Her neighbors viewed with suspicion the friendly relationships she was building with the occupying army. Boyd, however, insisted that these were simply the very beginnings of her efforts to collect information, which she would then pass on to benefit the Confederacy.

REBEL SPY

Boyd wrote down any information she learned from her Union admirers and then passed it on to either General Jeb Stuart or Stonewall Jackson. Much of this involved troop movements and plans for future military exercises. But Boyd was hardly skilled in spying. She made no attempt to disguise her messages, nor did she use any form of code.

A message eventually fell into Union hands, and Boyd's handwriting was quickly identified. She was summoned to Union headquarters and asked if she was aware that the punishment for treason was death. Instead of being frightened, Boyd boldly curtsied and sarcastically replied, "Thank you, gentlemen of the Jury," before leaving the room.

The Union had now officially identified Boyd as a possible spy, and so she had to be much more careful in her efforts to pass on information. She began to use messengers and became far more cautious about how information was sent. One of her messengers was an elderly African American, who carried a message hidden inside a watch whose insides had been removed. On at least one occasion she enlisted the help of a pretty friend, who walked seven miles (eleven km) to General Jackson's camp carrying information from Boyd.

News of other spies eventually reached Boyd. Soon she had made contact with Colonel Turner Ashby, a cavalry leader under Stonewall Jackson and head of the Confederate military scouts

Known for her fiery disposition, Belle Boyd grew from an inexperienced spy to a daring secret agent for the Confederacy. A natural charmer and flirt, Boyd simply listened as Union soldiers boasted of their battle plans and later relayed the information to her Confederate contact. Boyd was fearless in her spying and completely loyal to the Southern cause.

in the Shenandoah Valley. Battles were being fought throughout the region, and Boyd's skills on horseback were particularly useful as she traveled swiftly through the area, often on assignment from Ashby to serve as a messenger. She learned the use of code and became skillful at using charm and her eavesdropping skills to the benefit of the Confederacy.

Suspected of being a spy, Boyd was eventually searched by Federal officials and placed under arrest. She was, of course, carrying information, but she had hidden the most important documents on the African-American servant who was traveling with her. Once again her ability to charm helped her in the situation. She was taken by train to Baltimore and then to a comfortable hotel where she spent a week until she was finally released. Since no evidence against her could be found, she was simply given a friendly warning not to cause any trouble.

Boyd learned that her family was now in Front Royal, Virginia, where her aunt and uncle had a hotel. She decided to join them. Union forces had taken over the hotel, and her family was squeezed into a tiny cottage nearby. A young Union officer was stationed at the hotel, and as Boyd later reported, she soon received from him flowers, expressions of affection, poetry, and a great deal of very important information that she passed on to Confederate officials.

The Union officers stationed at the hotel unwisely boasted to Boyd of their upcoming plans to "whip" General Jackson, and told her the date of their departure. The night before they planned to leave, a meeting was held in the hotel. Boyd hid herself in a bedroom on the floor above. There was a small hole in the floor of the closet. Boyd lay on the closet floor, pressed her ear against the hole, and listened for several hours as the plans for the battle were discussed. When the meeting ended at 1:00 A.M., she crept back into the cottage where her family was staying and transcribed everything she had heard into code. She then went to the stable, saddled her horse, and galloped some 15 miles (25 km) to a home where her contact, Colonel Ashby, was staying. After giving him the information, she then made the two-hour journey back to her aunt's home, returning just before dawn.

On another occasion, Boyd heard that Confederate forces were advancing on Front Royal, and the worried Federal troops were scrambling, trying to hide their supplies and ammunition, planning to burn the bridge, and rallying troops to form a united front against the far larger Confederate force. Boyd asked several men who she knew were Southern sympathizers to carry

A Woman on the Battlefield

In the autobiographical *Belle Boyd in Camp and Prison*, Boyd recounted her adventures spying for the Confederacy. Although many of the accounts are undoubtedly exaggerated, Boyd nonetheless displays the excitement and challenges faced by those who spied during the Civil War. The book includes, among many other accounts, the following story of her efforts to deliver a critical message to Confederate troops in the midst of a battle at Front Royal:

> Upon this occasion my life was spared by what seemed to me then, and seems still, little short of a miracle; for, besides the numerous bullets that whistled by my ears, several actually pierced different parts of my clothing, but not one reached my body. Besides all this, I was exposed to a cross-fire from the Federal and Confederate artillery, whose shot and shell flew whistling and hissing over my head.
>
> At length a Federal shell struck the ground within 20 yards of my feet; and the explosion, of course, sent the fragments flying

the information to General Jackson, who was in command of the Confederate forces. They all refused. Finally, Boyd snatched up a sunbonnet and ran.

By now, the battle had begun. Boyd ran past the Union forces and out into the open field and beyond, toward the Confederate forces. Shells fell around her, and she scrambled and crawled her way along the edge of the field until she reached the advancing Confederate troops. The soldiers were astonished to see a woman rushing toward them, waving her sunbonnet. They were even more astonished when she reached them and

in every direction around me. I had, however, just time to throw myself flat upon the ground before the deadly engine burst; and again Providence spared my life.

Springing up when the danger was passed, I pursued my career, still under a heavy fire. I shall never run again as I ran on that, to me memorable day. Hope, fear, the love of life, and the determination to serve my country to the last, conspired to fill my heart with more than feminine courage, and to lend preternatural strength and swiftness to my limbs. I often marvel, and even shudder, when I reflect how I cleared the fields, and bounded over the fences with the agility of a deer.

As I neared our line I waved my bonnet to our soldiers, to intimate that they should press forward, upon which one regiment, the First Maryland "Rebel" Infantry, and Hay's Louisiana Brigade, gave me a loud cheer, and, without waiting for further orders, dashed upon the town at a rapid pace.

They did not then know who I was, and they were naturally surprised to see a woman on the battle-field, and on a spot, too, where the fire was so hot. Their shouts of approbation and triumph rang in my ears for many a day afterwards, and I still hear them not unfrequently in my dreams.

stammered out a message for General Jackson—that the Union force was very small and could easily be overtaken if he led an immediate charge. She then hurried back home.

Using her information, Jackson successfully led a charge on the Union troops, preventing them from burning the bridge and seizing their supplies. Confederates then chased them back northward toward the Potomac River. Jackson sent a grateful letter to Boyd, thanking her for her service.

In July 1862, Boyd was betrayed by a man with whom she had fallen in love, a man wearing the uniform of a Confederate soldier but who proved to be a spy for the Union forces. When Union officers came to her home, they found incriminating papers in a locked desk. She was arrested, moved to Washington, and imprisoned for a month in the Old Capitol Prison. From the window of her cell, she could see in the distance the home of Secretary Floyd, where she had enjoyed the life of a teenage debutante less than two years earlier.

IN PRISON

Northern newspapers gleefully published the story of the captured spy, but Boyd refused to confess anything and won the admiration of many of her fellow prisoners for singing and facing down her questioners with loud defiance. They communicated through holes in their cells, and friends who visited her smuggled in pictures of Jefferson Davis or Confederate flags that she proudly displayed in her cell. These displays of Confederate support resulted in punishment: confinement to her cell during the hottest days of the summer.

After a month of confinement, the 18-year-old Boyd was among a group released to Richmond in a prisoner exchange. Boyd was welcomed in Richmond, but when she tried to return to her family home in Martinsburg (then under Union control) she was once again arrested. This time she was held in Carroll

Jan. 14, 1860.] FRANK LESLIE'S ILLUSTRATED NEWSPAPER. 101

THE MOUNTAIN RANGERS, CAPT. ASHBY COMMANDING, SCOURING THE NEIGHBORHOOD OF CHARLESTOWN, VA., IN SEARCH OF SPIES, DURING THE HARPER'S FERRY INSURRECTION EXCITEMENT.—FROM A SKETCH MADE ON THE SPOT BY OUR OWN ARTIST.

An experienced rider since childhood, Belle Boyd learned to decipher and encode messages for Colonel Turner Ashby (left), a Confederate leader. One night, through a hole in the floor of her closet, Boyd overheard the entire Union military strategy for an upcoming battle. Determined to pass on this information to Colonel Ashby, Boyd rode fifteen miles in the middle of the night to deliver her findings to him.

Prison. After three months there, she caught typhoid fever and became very ill. After being warned not to enter Union territory again, she was released to Richmond.

While recovering from her own illness, Boyd learned that her father had died from an illness he caught while serving in the military. She decided to go abroad to recover, and took with her Confederate messages intended for England. Her ship set sail from Wilmington, North Carolina, the same city where Rose Greenhow had drowned after being chased by a Union ship. The *Greyhound*, with Boyd aboard, was also set upon by the Union fleet. The crew began tossing overboard many valuable bales of cotton (which they were transporting for sale in England) rather than have them fall into enemy hands. Money also was tossed into the sea, and Boyd burned the messages she was carrying.

The *Greyhound* was captured, its Confederate captain taken away for questioning, and the rest of the ship placed under the command of a Northern naval officer, Ensign Samuel Hardinge. In her memoir *Belle Boyd in Camp and Prison*, Boyd described him as a gentleman, whose "dark-brown hair hung down on his shoulders" and whose "eyes were large and bright." He did not immediately question her, but when he finally spoke with Boyd he asked her to consider herself a passenger rather than a prisoner.

The ship headed north. By the time the *Greyhound* reached Boston, Hardinge and Boyd were engaged. Unfortunately for Hardinge, Boyd and the Confederate captain of the *Greyhound* then escaped, with Boyd heading for Canada. Hardinge was held responsible, arrested, tried, and dismissed from the service.

IN LOVE WITH A YANKEE

In Canada, Boyd was able to arrange for transportation on a ship to England. After Hardinge's dismissal from the Navy, he traveled to England to find her. They were married in London in 1864.

Soon after the wedding, Hardinge decided to return to the United States. Some reports suggest that Boyd had converted him to the Confederate cause and that he was carrying documents intended for the Confederacy, but this has never been proved. What is known is that he spent time in Boston and with his family in Brooklyn before being arrested in Virginia under suspicion of being a spy. He was imprisoned, and when he finally returned to England he was suffering from an illness he had caught in prison. He died, leaving Boyd the mother of a young daughter and a widow at the age of 21.

Boyd sold whatever possessions she could in order to support herself and her daughter, and then published her memoir of the war, *Belle Boyd in Camp and Prison*, in London in 1865. Next, encouraged by a friend, she decided to pursue a career in theater. She made her debut in Manchester, England, in 1866, and by the end of the Civil War was able to return to the United States, where she continued to work in the theater.

In 1869, she married John Hammond, a businessman who had served as a Union officer. She had two daughters and a son with him, but the marriage ended in divorce in 1884. Soon after her divorce, she married a man 18 years younger than she was, Nathaniel Rice High. Finances were a problem for the couple, and Boyd began lecturing about her war experiences to earn money. She was particularly successful in the North, speaking to Union veterans and concluding her speeches with a dramatic plea for national unity.

In June 1900, while speaking before a group of veterans in Kilbourne, Wisconsin, she suffered a heart attack and died. She was 56 years old, and was buried at the Spring Grove Cemetery in Wisconsin. Four Union veterans carried her coffin. A small granite headstone at her grave bore the simple legend, a gift from a Confederate veteran:

BELLE BOYD
CONFEDERATE SPY
BORN IN VIRGINIA
DIED IN WISCONSIN
ERECTED BY A COMRADE.

African-American Spies

Some of the most valuable intelligence provided to Union troops during the Civil War was intelligence that came from African Americans. These include slaves who had run away, many of them after being forced to work in Confederate military camps. In addition, there was a stream of helpful intelligence provided by slaves who continued to work in homes and camps while secretly providing information to Union contacts. Other data was provided by African-American scouts and free blacks masquerading as slaves in order to slip behind Confederate lines.

The Confederate commander General Robert E. Lee suspected the source of much of the information that was being leaked to Union troops. By May 1863, he was warning his officers to use caution in the presence of slaves. But his warnings were made less effective by the prejudice that was part of a culture that permitted slavery. Slaves were so much a part of the labor throughout the South that they easily moved about without raising concern or alarm. In addition—and perhaps most importantly—they were largely ignored as part of the background of Confederate culture. Officers discussed the war or troop movements freely in front of them, without fear that the information would be understood or passed on to others.

Allan Pinkerton frequently used African Americans as scouts and informants when he was serving as General McClellan's intelligence chief. Under Pinkerton's direction, runaway slaves were carefully interviewed to determine what information they might have. Many were then recruited by Pinkerton to serve as scouts.

One of Pinkerton's more famous African-American scouts was John Scobell. Pinkerton recruited Scobell in the Fall of 1861. Scobell had been a slave in Mississippi. His owner was a Scotsman who educated Scobell and later freed him. Scobell's intelligence and skill at acting made him able to effectively masquerade as a cook, a laborer, or a servant (often as a servant to other Pinkerton agents).

As a team, Scobell and the other Pinkerton agents would gather separate bits of information. The white agents found out information from Confederate officers and officials, and Scobell gathered intelligence from leaders in black communities who might have information on local troop placements, fortifications, and conditions.

Some of Scobell's most valuable information involved intelligence on Confederate battle plans, the status of Confederate supplies, and the spirits of Confederate troops. Scobell was a member of the "Legal League," an underground slave organization whose goal involved using the Constitution and its legal protections to bring an end to slavery. At these meetings—held in the South—he gathered local information and also recruited other members to serve as informants or messengers.

Pinkerton also enlisted W.H. Ringgold as a spy. Ringgold was a free African American who had been forced to work on a Virginia riverboat that was transporting Confederate troops and supplies. Ringgold and other crewmembers spent six

African-American spies contributed a great deal of information to the Union army during the Civil War. Allan Pinkerton, the head of the Union's secret police, employed African Americans, many of whom proved to be talented actors, to masquerade as slaves in the South or servants of his undercover agents. Above, Pinkerton and some of his men, including an unidentified African-American man in the foreground.

months on the riverboat before they were allowed to return to the North. Pinkerton interviewed Ringgold and received from him detailed information about Confederate fortifications along the Virginia peninsula.

George Scott was another valuable spy. Scott was a runaway slave who had escaped from a plantation near Yorktown,

Virginia. He made his way to the Union-held Fort Monroe, on the James River near the tip of the Virginia peninsula. Along the way, Scott noticed that Confederate troops had put up two large fortifications between Yorktown and the fort.

When he reached the fort, Scott told the Union officers what he had seen. They demanded confirmation of the information, so Scott agreed to go back with a Union officer to show him the fortifications and gather additional intelligence. On one scouting mission, Confederate forces shot at Scott. He was uninjured, but a bullet did tear a hole in his jacket.

As a result of Scott's scouting missions, General Benjamin Butler, the commander of Fort Monroe, learned that Confederate forces were planning an attack on Newport News, Virginia, in order to cut off Fort Monroe from Union supplies. Butler responded with an attack on Confederate forces, but the operation was not well planned and ended in Union defeat.

SPY IN THE WHITE HOUSE

One of the boldest African-American spies was a former servant of Elizabeth Van Lew, the Union informant in Richmond. The Van Lew family had owned 21 slaves in 1850. By 1860, they only had two, both of whom were elderly women. But the Van Lews had not undertaken the legal process of formally freeing their slaves. Under Virginia law, freed slaves must leave Virginia within a year. It was this technicality that allowed Elizabeth Van Lew to enlist her former slave, Mary Bowser, as a spy for the Union.

The Van Lews' treatment of Mary Bowser had long been a source of some controversy among Richmond's wealthiest families. After Elizabeth Van Lew's father had died, she and her mother had arranged for Bowser, then known as Mary Jane Richards, to be baptized in their church, St. John's Episcopal Church, the site of Patrick Henry's famous "Give me liberty or give me death" speech. The uncommon treatment of Richards continued still later, when she was sent away to Philadelphia to be educated at a Quaker school for black students. This was at a time when it was a crime in many parts of the South to teach a slave to read and write. In 1855, she sailed to Liberia, an African nation founded by Americans as a colony for ex-slaves. It seems clear from this that the Van Lews intended for Richards to remain in freedom in Africa.

But five years later, in March 1860, Richards returned by boat from Africa. Landing in Baltimore, she then traveled back to Richmond, in defiance of the law that ordered freed slaves to be exiled from Virginia. Five months later she was arrested in Richmond and put in jail. Elizabeth Van Lew then paid a fine and stated that Richards had not broken any law because she was, in fact, still a slave.

Richards married, and became Mary Elizabeth Bowser. Elizabeth Van Lew next arranged to place Mary Bowser in a critical location: the home in Richmond where the president of the Confederacy, Jefferson Davis, lived and maintained his executive office, known as the Richmond White House. Used to ignoring the presence of slaves, Davis paid little attention to Bowser as she went about her daily duties. He exercised little caution in protecting official documents left on his desk—slaves, after all, were legally supposed to be illiterate.

But Bowser had been educated in Philadelphia, and had an extra talent—a photographic memory. As she dusted Davis's office, she was able to memorize the military documents placed there and later repeat them word for word. Similarly, she was able to pass on the content of conversations she overheard while serving in the dining room.

Bowser's role as a servant allowed her to disguise the information she was carrying. A basket of eggs could contain one empty shell filled with details of military plans. The serving tray she carried had a false bottom and might be loaded with food on top and secret messages hidden below. Even the laundry was a means of communication: A white shirt hung to dry beside an upside-down pair of pants signaled that troops were being moved to the West.

More than a hundred years passed before Bowser's contribution to the Union was formally recognized. In 1995, Mary Bowser was admitted to the U.S. Army Intelligence Hall of Fame.

Civil War Heroine

On July 18, 1863, the Boston newspaper *The Commonwealth* published an article on its front page detailing the exploits of Harriet Tubman and her team during their surprise raid on a Confederate depot, an excerpt of which is published below:

> Col. Montgomery and his gallant band of 300 black soldiers, under the guidance of a black woman, dashed into the enemy's country, struck a bold and effective blow, destroying millions of dollars worth of commissary stores, cotton and lordly dwellings, and striking terror into the heart of rebeldom, brought off near 800 slaves and thousands of dollars worth of property, without losing a man or receiving a scratch. . . .
>
> The Colonel was followed by a speech from the black woman, who led the raid and under whose inspiration it was originated and conducted. For sound sense and real native eloquence, her address would do honor to any man, and it created a great sensation. . . .
>
> Since the rebellion she has devoted herself to her great work of delivering the bondman, with an energy and sagacity [wisdom] that cannot be exceeded. Many and many times she has penetrated the enemy's lines and discovered their situation and condition, and escaped without injury, but not without extreme hazard. . . .

Source: www.harriettubman.com.

Bowser was not the only member of Jefferson Davis's household who provided valuable information to the Union. William A. Jackson was another slave hired by Davis to work as a servant. In Jackson's case, he was hired as Davis's coachman.

Like Bowser, Jackson was largely ignored as Davis went about his official business, often holding conversations about political and military matters in front of the coachman. Jackson then traveled behind Union lines to pass on information he had overheard.

The first recorded report made by Jackson took place on May 3, 1862, after he had crossed Union lines near Fredericksburg, Virginia. The specifics of the intelligence Jackson provided were not recorded, but what is known is that the information was considered so vital that it was immediately telegraphed to the Department of War in Washington.

HARRIET TUBMAN

Many people are familiar with Harriet Tubman's work on the Underground Railroad leading slaves to freedom in the North. Among her lesser-known accomplishments is her work as a Civil War spy along the coast of South Carolina.

Tubman was born Harriet Ross, a slave in Maryland, in either 1819 or 1820. As a young girl she was beaten by her owners and suffered a head injury at the age of 15 that resulted in recurring headaches and seizures. She married John Tubman, a free African American, when she was 25 years old. Four years later, afraid that she would be sold, she escaped to freedom, leaving behind the husband who refused to go with her.

Abolitionists had set up the Underground Railroad as a network of volunteers to help slaves on their way to freedom. Tubman used the Underground Railroad to travel to the North. She later became its most famous "conductor." Through her many trips back and forth between the North and South she delivered some 300 slaves to freedom.

Harriet Tubman established her own spy network during the Civil War. With the help of local people who knew the area, Tubman alerted Union forces to Confederate weak points, supplies, and camp movements. Tubman proved to be effective and was allowed to join a raid on a Confederate supply depot.

When the Civil War began, Tubman discovered that her work on the Underground Railroad was no longer possible. Instead, she found a new calling. As Union troops advanced into Maryland in early 1861, many black slaves rushed out to join them. They were officially labeled "contraband of war," and the information they provided was often referred to as "contraband information" in official documents of the time. Although they were no longer slaves, they were also not officially free. Lincoln's Emancipation Proclamation, which freed Southern slaves, did not take effect until January 1, 1863.

Tubman soon learned that Union forces needed help caring for these escaped slaves. She traveled south to Maryland, helping to clothe and feed those who had sought protection within Union camps.

When Union forces captured Port Royal in South Carolina, many plantation owners fled before the advancing army, abandoning their slaves. These slaves were often sick and undernourished, and they soon began to pour into the Union camps. An order was sent out requesting nurses and teachers to care for these people. Tubman responded by traveling to South Carolina in March 1862. She worked as a nurse for both the former slaves and for white soldiers injured in the region. She attempted to find work for those who had been slaves. There was a need for medicine, clothing, and supplies, but soon Tubman became aware of another need: spies.

Tubman quickly put together a unit of ex-slaves who knew the region well. Some of these were men who had served as riverboat pilots and were quite familiar with the waterways that marked South Carolina's coast. Many of the river mouths and waterways were patrolled by Union river craft, and Tubman's unit was charged with finding mines that had been placed there. They gathered additional information and eventually Tubman's work evolved into a kind of guerilla warfare.

One of Tubman's most famous missions occurred on the night of June 2, 1863, when she and Colonel James Montgomery

led a force of 150 African-American soldiers up the Comba-
hee River in three steam-powered gunboats. They successfully
avoided the mines that Tubman's men had spotted, and then
headed on to the shore, destroying a Confederate supply depot,
setting fire to homes and warehouses and rounding up some
750 slaves. The Boston newspaper *The Commonwealth* of July
18, 1863, described the successful mission and praised the efforts of Tubman, noting, "many times she has penetrated the
enemy's lines and discovered their situation and condition, and
escaped without injury, but not without extreme hazard."

Divided Loyalties

The experience of Elizabeth Van Lew, a Union sympathizer living in Richmond, was not unique. Many families still loyal to the Union found themselves on the wrong side of the secession line when the Civil War broke out. Often they chose to keep their sympathies secret, quietly passing on information or aid when possible. Others chose to serve in the Union Army, leaving their families behind in Southern territory.

David Strother offers an interesting example of the latter. Strother was born in Martinsburg, Virginia, in 1816. His father had been a lieutenant in the U.S. Army during the War of 1812 and later served as a colonel in the Virginia militia. Strother, however, was unsuccessful in his efforts to win an appointment to West Point Military Academy. Instead he attended college in Pennsylvania for a year and then studied art, first in New York and later in Paris, Florence, and Rome. He returned home and became a book illustrator before taking on an assignment for *Harper's Weekly* as a correspondent.

Traveling through the North and South on various assignments, Strother began to appreciate the connections that knitted the country together and the importance of preserving the Union. As war threatened in the 1850s, his growing belief was that the South could not survive independent of the North.

Yet Strother was very critical of abolitionism, and when war came, he returned to Virginia, intending to remain neutral. But few could remain neutral in the heat of civil war, and Strother joined the Union Army in July 1861 as a civilian topographer, creating maps that showed the physical features of the areas through which he traveled.

In the early days of the war, Strother was often asked to review intelligence provided by escaped slaves and local informants. He quickly grew exasperated with the misinformation circulating in Virginia, as expressed in his Civil War journals, later published in serial form in *Harper's* magazine from 1866 to 1868 under the title *Personal Recollections of the War*.

As Strother noted in one journal entry from March 1862, he was amazed at how strongly people in the South felt about a cause that he described as "desperate":

> There is nothing too absurd for them to accept on the one side or too plain for them to reject on the other. I have never seen the human mind so enslaved by desire. They meet together in little knots to discuss flank movements and the grand strategy of falling back on somewhere. If a loyal man [one who supported the Union] approaches them they are silent or disperse. Day by day the silliest and most improbable stories of Confederate victories are circulated. They count every troop and cannon that passes and underrate the force as much as possible. It is droll and at the same time sad and humiliating.

LOUISIANA LOYALIST

There were Unionists—people who remained loyal to the U.S. government—all throughout the South. As is clear from the story of David Strother, an opposition to slavery was not always what motivated this loyalty. Instead, there were complex factors that determined whether someone living in the South supported the idea of secession or instead remained supportive of the Union.

Their response to the war was equally complex. Some Southerners who were loyal to the Union chose to enlist in the Union Army. Others engaged in a kind of guerrilla war, secretly attacking Confederate depots and in other ways attempting to disrupt the Confederate efforts. Still others chose to practice active resistance, ultimately serving as scouts and spies for the Union.

Dennis E. Haynes chose this route, first attempting to resist when his state joined the Confederacy and later serving as a scout for Union forces. Haynes was an Irish immigrant who had been born in Dublin in 1819. He immigrated to the United States with two of his brothers in the early 1830s, married, and worked either as a grocer or lawyer (the records differ) in Georgia.

In the 1850s, he traveled to Nicaragua, serving as an engineer there before returning to the United States and ultimately moving with his family to Texas. He was in Texas in 1861 when support for secession swept through the state. Haynes was outspoken in his opposition to secession and his neighbors viewed him as an "outlaw" because of his beliefs. Haynes at one point worked to organize a company of men to serve in the Union Army, but Confederate forces tried to arrest the group and Haynes went into hiding.

While in hiding, Haynes learned that a large Federal force had reached Alexandria, Louisiana, under the command of Major General Nathaniel Banks. Haynes decided to go to Louisiana to see if he could persuade Banks to lead an expedition into eastern Texas so Unionists there could escape to safety under the protection of the Union Army. But on the way to Alexandria, Haynes learned that Federal forces had evacuated

Colonel David H. Strother was an artist and journalist who enlisted in the Federal army during the Civil War. Working under the pseudonym Porte Crayon, Strother created illustrations and reported on events for Harper's Illustrated, *a popular newspaper of the time. Strother developed a deep love for the United States while traveling on assignment for his work, and despite his Southern roots, he supported the Union during the war.*

the town. At that point, he chose to remain where he was, some 30 miles (50 km) from Alexandria.

Haynes acquired a farm in Louisiana, but eventually his neighbors learned of his support for the Union and alerted the Confederates. It was a time when Louisianans sympathetic to the Union were engaging in guerrilla war (they called their military units "Jayhawkers") and Confederate forces were actively trying to stamp out any Jayhawkers or Unionists in the region. As a Unionist, Haynes was seen as a threat to the Confederacy and he was arrested, along with one of his sons.

Haynes escaped and made his way home, where he and two of his sons hid in the swamps and then in the home of a fellow Unionist. By February 1864, Haynes had decided to travel to Union territory and offer his services as a scout and spy. He went to New Orleans, where he learned that the Union forces under the command of General Banks were planning an attack on Alexandria.

Haynes was hired first to provide information about the region and those who would likely support the Union. Later, he was given an assignment to slip through the swamps and make contact with those he knew or suspected might be Unionists, and to recruit them for the army. He was able to enlist more than a hundred men. The campaign ultimately proved a failure, however, and Haynes and the other scouts retreated with the army toward the Mississippi River. He soon came down with typhoid fever and was discharged from the army on July 16, 1864. After the war, he served in local politics and continued to face prejudice and threats of violence from those who had supported the Confederacy.

In 1866, Haynes published an account of his experiences, titled *A Thrilling Narrative of the Sufferings of Union Refugees, and the Massacre of the Martyrs of Liberty of Western Louisiana: Together with a Brief Sketch of the Present Political Status of Louisiana, As to her Unfitness for Admission into the Union. With Letters to the Governor of Louisiana and Noted Secessionists in*

That State, and a Letter to President Johnson on Reconstruction. As the title suggests, Haynes's focus was not merely on providing an account of those who had suffered as Unionists in Confederate Louisiana nor on his role as a scout and spy for the Union Army. It also focused on his anger at the return to political power, after the war, of many of the men who had actively worked against the Union.

Haynes included in his memoir a copy of a letter sent to Andrew Johnson, president of the United States, on December 30, 1865, describing the hardships he had suffered as a scout for the Union Army after returning home to Louisiana. His home had been burned, and his possessions stolen. He was also threatened with personal harm. Many former scouts and spies could not leave their homes except in large, well-armed groups. Haynes noted that these former scouts, spies, and refugees had returned home to be "first received with scowls, and after a little, as your Excellency showed clemency in pardoning the most notorious of those traitors, they became bolder, and publicly declared that as soon as the Federal army . . . are withdrawn, they intend to run off all the Union men, and more especially the scouts who took up arms against them."

YANKEES IN ATLANTA

As Haynes's account makes clear, spies and informants faced danger both during the war and well after it had ended. Those who chose to support a different side from their neighbors faced harsh criticism and often became social outcasts long after the military campaign of the Civil War was over.

Cyrena Stone was a Unionist living in Atlanta whose diaries tell of a small circle of "Secret Yankees" who chose to remain loyal to the Union, despite the danger they faced if their sympathies became public. She was born Cyrena Bailey in East Berkshire, Vermont, in 1830 and grew up in a series of small Vermont and New York villages where her father served as a Congregationalist minister. In August 1850, she married a young lawyer, Amherst Willoughby Stone, who moved his bride to Fayetteville, Georgia, some 25 miles (40 km) from Atlanta. Their only child, a little girl named Jennie, died soon after her first birthday. Shortly after her death, the Stones moved to Atlanta.

Amherst Stone's legal practice flourished in the booming economy of Atlanta, and Cyrena began publishing religious and spiritual essays in several Atlanta newspapers and magazines. The couple soon became part of some of the city's most prominent social groups. Amherst was chosen as president of the Bank of Fulton, the first bank in the city organized and run by local residents. They purchased a stately home on 10 acres (4 hectares) and by 1860 the couple owned six slaves. They, like many Southerners, called their slaves "servants."

By the 1860s, the Stones, despite their mixing into Atlanta society, were still viewed as Yankees. In 1861, the slaves' ownership was legally transferred from Amherst to Cyrena. Amherst likely feared that, as a Unionist, his property might be taken away under Confederate law.

The number of Unionists in Atlanta when the Stones first arrived is unknown, but it is certain that no more than 100 families would describe themselves as Unionists once the Civil War began. Following the presidential campaign of 1860, anger toward Northerners in Atlanta increased. A small group of Unionist men, among them Amherst Stone, were soon meeting in secret to discuss politics. They later met to discuss ways to avoid being drafted into the Confederate Army.

Despite the secret meetings, Amherst Stone made several public speeches arguing against Georgia seceding from the Union. His speeches did not change the course of action, as Georgia seceded from the Union in January 1861. Immediately, the atmosphere in Atlanta changed. Many who had supported the Union instead declared themselves in favor of secession or quietly maintained a position of neutrality. The reasons for this were obvious: Anyone outspoken in their support for the Union could have been whipped or lynched and would certainly be forced to leave Georgia.

Thomas G. Dyer's *Secret Yankees* notes that, as war threatened, the Atlanta newspaper the *Intelligencer* urged its readers to "Look out for Spies." The paper warned that the "Black Republican Government" of Lincoln had sent secret agents to inform on events in Atlanta to "our Northern enemies." Unionists came under increased suspicion: It was believed that they were spies or they were helping the spies who came to Atlanta.

It was a complex time. Amherst Stone's brother Chester, who had moved with him from Vermont to Georgia, lived nearby and was also becoming active in Atlanta society. Chester Stone decided to side with the Confederacy and joined a militia unit fighting Union forces. Despite their political differences the brothers remained close, and Cyrena in her diaries movingly describes Chester's departure for war while knowing "that he was going to fight against the land of their birth, perhaps their own kindred."

In late spring and early summer of 1862, Union prisoners began arriving in Atlanta. Their conditions were often shocking, and local citizens gathered around the prisons to taunt them. Cyrena Stone began visiting some prisoners, bringing them food or money. Her activities raised suspicion, particularly as warnings about spies and a potential slave revolt spread through Atlanta. Finally, Cyrena was brought before a military court for questioning. She was asked about secret societies supporting the Union in Atlanta and questioned about possible plans to overthrow the Confederacy. Then she was released.

By October, the Confederacy expanded the age limit of men eligible to serve in the army. Men as old as 45 were now included. Amherst Stone was then 36, and he began to make arrangements to leave Atlanta and make his way northward, taking as much of his wealth with him as he could. He then planned to arrange for safe passage for his wife. Stone traveled to New York and then went on to Vermont to visit family. While in New York, he sent several telegrams arranging for ships to run the Union blockade and transport a large supply of cotton to the North for sale. It was a foolish action that quickly led to his arrest as a spy and smuggler. He was transported to a military prison in New York Harbor and charged with serving as an agent of the Confederate government. He was held with several dozen other prisoners in a damp and dark cell about 14 feet long and 24 feet wide (4 m long and 7 m wide). Among his fellow prisoners were at least eight Confederate officers, including the son of Robert E. Lee. Stone quickly adapted to the situation, making friends with his fellow prisoners as one more Southerner victimized by the dreaded Yankees.

Stone was held in prison for about two months before he was able to bribe his way to freedom. It had been a tricky situation—describing himself as a Unionist to the authorities while convincing his cellmates of his loyalty to the Confederacy—but he had succeeded.

Over the course of the next few months, Stone traveled to Washington, D.C., making arrangements with federal authorities for the ship containing cotton and the rest of his assets to run the blockade. He also arranged for his wife to safely be transported from Atlanta. He obtained a pass to return to the South, and upon receiving it he gratefully passed along some intelligence he had found out from an informant who had traveled to the North to avoid being drafted into the Confederate Army. The information reported on a massing of Confederate militia at Dalton, 38 miles (60 km) south of Chattanooga, with details of Lee's army's plans to evacuate Charleston and move toward Dalton.

Stone did not want to be named as the source of the intelligence but somehow he was. He learned that he had been named as an informant and spy and traveled first to Tennessee rather than Georgia. Stone would later state that Cyrena warned him

Union supporters living in the South often were forced to hide their allegiances to protect themselves from those who supported the Rebel cause. Some of those who were pro-Union participated in guerrilla tactics and served as scouts (above) and spies for the North. Others, like Cyrena Stone, stayed in the South and set up a network of like-minded people.

against returning to Atlanta. Instead he returned to New York. Ironically, he was again arrested, this time for bribing his way out of prison, and was held in prison for several months under suspicion of anti-Union activity. Stone's experiences outline the climate of suspicion in both the North and South. Anyone could

The Sounds of Battle

Cyrena Stone kept a diary of her experiences as a Unionist in Atlanta. The following account is from midnight, July 21, 1864, reprinted in *Secret Yankees* by Thomas G. Dyer. In it, Stone reveals the chaos of the city as Union troops advanced and Confederate forces attempted to defend the city:

> Words cannot picture the scenes that surround me—scenes & sounds which my soul will hold in remembrance forever. Terrific cannonading on every side—continual firing of musketry—men screaming to each other—wagons rumbling by on every street, or pouring into the yard—for the few remnants of fences—offers no obstructions new to cavalryman or wagoner,—and from the city comes up wild shouting, as if there was a general melee there.
>
> I sit in my dismantled home tonight, feeling that our earthly loves, and all our pleasant things, are ours so slightly. Am in this little parlor where quiet, happy hours have glided by, as I thought & dreamed;—where in other sabbath twilights we used to sing the dear old sacred songs; where have been social joys & pleasant communings, and friend clasped the hand of friend in true companionship of soul. And to night? Ah—I stand alone on a now desolate island, where my heart had always a summer, & life seemed one radiant morning! Alone—& reaching out my hands in vain, as the red waves of War rush madly by—sweeping away our pleasant Home.

be suspected of being a spy, even—in Stone's case—a spy both for the Union and the Confederacy.

ATLANTA HOSTESS

Meanwhile, back in Atlanta, Cyrena continued to meet with friends and manage as best she could in her husband's absence.

The Union spy Émile Bourlier came to Atlanta in September 1863 looking for information about Confederate troop movements and Confederate morale. At some point he managed to make contact with the few Unionists in Atlanta, among them, Cyrena Stone. At her home he supposedly met with other Unionists, who shared their thoughts on the war. Bourlier is one of several Union spies thought to have had contact with Cyrena Stone during the war. Later, she herself was accused of providing intelligence to the Federals, but she would deny that, even in her diary.

By July 1864, as the Federals advanced on Atlanta, many of Cyrena Stone's friends had fled the city. She was one of the few still in the neighborhood. She even gave shelter to an injured Confederate colonel when the fighting was particularly fierce. Other Confederate soldiers offered her protection while the battle raged nearby, helping her to pack up many of her belongings when it seemed likely that she would need to evacuate. On July 22, 1864, she was finally forced from her home. When the Union Army marched into Atlanta, Stone was one of a crowd that stood on the streets. She stood for about two hours waving a silk Union flag, and the soldiers who saw her responded with cheers.

DUTY AND HONOR

The federal troops whom Stone had cheered as they entered Atlanta would ultimately destroy most of the city. She finally rejoined her husband and they settled in Savannah, where he became a prominent Republican politician during Reconstruction, describing himself firmly as a committed abolitionist. But there was little acceptance in Savannah for those known to have been loyal to the Union during the war, and Cyrena spent more and more time with her family in Vermont. She died at the age of 38 in Vermont, far from her husband, in December 1868.

Amherst Stone served in local politics in Georgia, remarried, and in 1873 was appointed a U.S. judge in Colorado, when it was still a territory. His two brothers also settled there—one a Confederate veteran, one a Union veteran. He spent the rest of his life in Colorado, dying at the age of 74.

The stories of the Stones, David Strother, and Dennis Haynes all show the challenges and dangers facing those who remained loyal to the Union while living in the South. Many found themselves providing some sort of intelligence, whether accidental or deliberate. Others offered support or assistance to those who were spying. They faithfully supported the return of the South to the Union and often encountered great difficulty and hardship for their loyalty and service long after the war had ended.

Spies in Disguise

During the Civil War, women played a variety of critical roles. Many managed family farms and businesses while the men were serving in the military. Others served as nurses, caring for the wounded in the makeshift hospitals set up near battle sites. Still others served as messengers and spies. Among the most intriguing stories of women's service in the Civil War are of those who disguised themselves as male soldiers, either to serve in the military or to work as a spy—or both. Mary Elizabeth Massey, in her book *Women in the Civil War*, estimates that some 400 women served in both armies as soldiers, while others followed husbands, sons, or fathers to the front, and still others acted as spies.

Among the women who assumed a disguise to aid in intelligence gathering was Pauline Cushman. She was born in New Orleans in 1833. At the age of 18, she left home and traveled to New York to pursue a career in the theater, and eventually she toured the United States, performing in different playhouses.

Union officials realized they could use Pauline Cushman, an actress with a pro-Confederate reputation, to flirt with and tease information out of Rebel soldiers. Though she was initially successful, Confederate forces began to suspect her of spying when plans discussed in her presence were leaked to Union forces.

By 1862, Cushman was a struggling actress working in a theater in Louisville. In the play, her character was required to give a toast. On one occasion she was dared to give the toast to the president of the Confederacy, Jefferson Davis. Cushman agreed, but first sought the permission of the local authorities. After receiving permission, Cushman made the toast. But when the theater manager learned of her actions, he promptly fired her, accusing her of being a Confederate sympathizer.

Cushman's skills as an actress and her reputation as a Southern sympathizer made her a natural as a spy. She was approached by one of the Union officials who had given permission for her to make the toast in the first place, and within a few months, the well-dressed Cushman was seen in Confederate camps. She flirted with Confederate officers in Kentucky and Tennessee and obtained valuable information, which she then passed on to Union contacts.

Gradually, Cushman's visibility in the camps made people suspicious, particularly when plans discussed in her presence were frequently leaked to Union sources. She was searched and discovered with incriminating papers. A military court sentenced her to death by hanging, but Cushman fell ill before the sentence could be carried out. When the Confederate forces moved out, Cushman was left behind and was finally rescued by Union forces at Shelbyville, Tennessee. She traveled to the North, where President Abraham Lincoln gave her the honorary commission of major. She spent several years traveling around the country, wearing her honorary uniform and telling stories of her adventures as a spy.

DIFFERENT ALIASES

Sarah Emma Edmonds wore several different disguises in her work as a spy for the Union. Unlike Cushman, Edmonds's skills depended on her ability to blend in, almost unnoticed, no matter the setting. At times Edmonds disguised herself as an African-American slave or a male soldier.

Edmonds was born in Nova Scotia in 1842. Fleeing an abusive father, Edmonds traveled south to the United States, eventually settling in Flint, Michigan. She became fiercely loyal to her adopted country, and when she first learned that the Union needed soldiers, she decided to enlist. She cut her hair, bought a man's suit, and was accepted as a male nurse in the U.S. Army in 1861, using the alias Frank Thompson.

How was it possible for women like Sarah Emma Edmonds to successfully enlist in the army as men? At the time, army recruitment exams asked potential recruits several questions about their occupation and their reason for enlisting. There was generally no physical exam. There was no intensive period of training or boot camp. Soldiers lived outside, and could slip away from camp to wash or handle other sanitary matters. Clothing was loose and often fit poorly, enabling women to more easily disguise themselves.

After a brief period of training in Washington, D.C., Edmonds's unit was sent south as part of General McClellan's campaign in Virginia. Edmonds was preparing to serve as a male nurse in the hospital unit when she learned that McClellan's staff was looking for volunteers to serve as spies before the campaign began. Edmonds, masquerading as Private Frank Thompson, volunteered.

To serve as a spy, the already disguised Edmonds assumed yet another disguise, this time as an African-American man. She darkened her skin, put on a wig and the kind of clothing a slave might wear, and slipped into Confederate territory.

Edmonds was quickly drafted to help a group of slaves charged with building defenses against the expected attack from McClellan's forces. The manual labor was not something Edmonds was used to, and after the first day her hands were so blistered that she was in agony. She persuaded a slave to switch jobs with her, and she took his place in the kitchen of the military camp, where she soon gathered valuable information about the morale of the Confederate forces, the size of the army, and the

Weaver in Georgia

Union spy Nora Winder traveled through the South, often accompanied by her young son, reporting on information she gathered. Disguised as a weaver, a valuable skill in the Confederacy, she earned money and also obtained useful information from the families who hired her.

In a letter to Major General William T. Sherman from February 12, 1865, Winder reports on what she learned while on assignment in Georgia: Confederate officer Lt. General John Bell Hood was resigning and being replaced by Lt. General Richard Taylor. Her letter read:

Honorable Sir:

. . . I will write you the most important news I know. I left Milledgeville the 25th of November . . . and came to Augusta. I arrived at that place the 28th of November. Augusta was in a great excitement at that time . . . [in preparation for being] evacuated, and then surrendered. There were 3,000 men sent on Brier Creek at Ellison's Bridge, and all the rest of the forces [about 5,000 men] were sent through South Carolina to Savannah. . . .

I remained in Augusta . . . for two weeks. Then I came to Warren County and remained there three days. During that time I saw about 200 wagons or more, all going to Gordon to haul supplies to Mayfield to be sent by railroad to North Carolina and Virginia. . . . [O]n the 30th of January my son . . . and myself started out on foot for Savannah. . . . I heard it rumored that Hood's army was near Augusta and coming on. I did not see a man from Hood's army. I saw and read a letter myself from one of Hood's men to his wife, an acquaintance of mine. . . . He wrote that Hood's army was cut all to pieces. There was not a horse saved. They lost all their cannon, but saved the carriages which bore up the guns. He also said Hood have [sic] given up his command to Dick Taylor. . . .

Source: *J. Matthew Gallman, ed.,* The Civil War Chronicle *(New York: Crown Publishers, 2000).*

weapons it possessed. She even was able to note the position of so-called "Quaker guns," logs painted black to make them look like cannons from a distance. She then slipped back into Union territory and passed on the information she had gathered to McClellan's staff before returning to work as a male nurse.

Within two months, she was again given an assignment to spy. This time, she disguised herself as an Irish peddler woman. She traveled through the Confederate camp, selling wares and gathering more information.

Edmonds made several more spying expeditions, assuming different disguises. Once, disguised as an African-American laundress, she discovered official military papers in the pocket of a Confederate officer's coat and was able to carry them back to the Union officers. On another occasion, disguised as a young man sympathetic to the Confederate cause, she linked up with a group serving as Confederate spies in Louisville. She was able to provide details of the group's membership when she returned to the Union camp.

In 1863, Edmonds caught malaria. She knew that if she checked herself into a military hospital her true identity as a woman would be revealed. So instead, she traveled to Cairo, Illinois, this time dressed as a woman, and checked into a private hospital. She planned to recover and then resume her identity as Frank Thompson, but while in Illinois she saw the name "Frank Thompson" listed on an army bulletin as a deserter. She knew then that Frank Thompson's military career—and spying career—must come to an end.

Instead, Edmonds returned to Washington and served as a nurse—a female nurse—until the war ended. She then published a successful memoir, *Nurse and Spy in the Union Army*. But Edmonds's status as a deserter continued to trouble her. Finally, she petitioned the Department of War to review her case. In July 1884, the U.S. Congress granted Sarah Emma Edmonds, alias Frank Thompson, an honorable discharge from the army and a veteran's pension of $12 per month.

DOCTOR AND SPY

Mary Edwards Walker is the only woman to have earned the Congressional Medal of Honor for her service in the Civil War. She was born in Oswego, New York, in 1832. Her father was a doctor and abolitionist who believed in equality for his five daughters. In an extraordinary action for the time, she enrolled in medical school—the only woman in her class—and received a doctor of medicine degree in 1855. At the time, she was only the second woman to graduate from a medical school in the United States. She went into private practice in Rome, New York, with her husband, another doctor, but both the practice and the marriage floundered. The couple divorced after 13 years of marriage.

When war broke out, Walker traveled to Washington to try to join the army. She was denied a commission as a medical officer but volunteered anyway, becoming the first female surgeon in the U.S. Army. As an unpaid volunteer she served first in the U.S. Patent Hospital in Washington and later as a field surgeon near the Union front lines.

She believed that traditional female clothing was too tight and uncomfortable, so she adopted a modified version of a male officer's uniform to wear while traveling with the army and working in field hospitals. While serving as assistant surgeon for the 52nd Ohio Infantry, she began her work as a spy, traveling across Confederate lines to treat civilians and gather valuable information.

In 1864, Confederate forces captured Walker. She was held as a prisoner of war in Richmond for four months before finally becoming part of a prisoner exchange with 24 other Union doctors. Walker then returned to the 52nd Ohio Infantry, but for the remainder of the war she practiced at a Louisville women's prison and at a home for orphans in Tennessee. After the war, she became a noted lecturer on women's rights and health issues. She was outspoken about the evils of alcohol and tobacco and was arrested more than once for wearing men's clothing as part of her campaign to urge reform in the dress code for women.

In 1865, Walker was awarded the Congressional Medal of Honor by President Andrew Johnson. The award was withdrawn in 1917, along with 910 other medals, when the standards for awarding the medal were revised by Congress to include only "actual combat with an enemy." Walker refused to give back the medal, wearing it every day until her death in 1919. It was not until 1977 that the U.S. Army officially recognized her medal once again.

CUBAN CONFEDERATE

The story of Loreta Janeta Velazquez is another fascinating story of a woman who assumed a man's identity and served in the Civil War, this time as a Confederate soldier. Velazquez was born in Cuba in 1842. She was the daughter of a Spanish official and was sent to New Orleans to further her education. Instead, she ran away, met an officer in the U.S. Army, and married him in 1856.

The couple had three children, all of whom died at a young age. When the Civil War began, Velazquez's sympathies were firmly on the side of the Confederacy. Both she and her father-in-law (a Texan) persuaded her husband to resign his commission in the U.S. Army. Finally, he agreed, joining the Confederate forces.

Her husband left the couple's home city of Memphis to join the Confederate forces in Richmond. Shortly afterward, Velazquez decided that she, too, wanted to serve. Working with a tailor who kept her secret safe, she cleverly designed and made a series of undergarments to conceal her shape and prepared to join the Confederate forces as Harry T. Buford. As she wrote in her memoir *The Woman in Battle*, published in 1876:

> With such underwear as I used, any woman who can disguise her features can readily pass for a man, and deceive the closest observers. So many men have weak and feminine voices that, provided the clothing is properly constructed and put on right, and the disguise in other respects is well arranged, a woman with even a very high-pitched voice need have very little to fear on that score.

Mary Edwards Walker refused to accept societal limitations for women and became one of the first female doctors in the United States. She volunteered for the Union and was awarded the Medal of Honor by President Andrew Johnson for her achievements during the war. Although the honor was later revoked due to a Congressional decision, Walker continued to wear her medal illegally (above).

Adding a false mustache to her disguise, Velazquez began her service by recruiting a group of young men to join the Confederate Army. This private militia then traveled to New Orleans, where it joined a Confederate force marching to Alabama.

During this expedition, Velazquez learned that her husband had been killed accidentally during a training exercise, when a weapon he was demonstrating exploded. Velazquez turned over command of her militia to a friend of her late husband, Captain De Caulp, who led them on to Pensacola, Florida. Velazquez wanted to be closer to the front and traveled with a group of other soldiers moving toward Richmond.

Velazquez arrived in time to serve in the Battle of Bull Run, but found the periods of inactivity between battles to be unbearable. She finally decided to serve as a spy, this time disguising herself as a female servant. She borrowed clothing and traveled north to Washington. She took careful note of the soldiers stationed around Washington. Once in the city, she made contact with friends of her husband who had served with him in the U.S. Army and were now stationed as part of the Federal force protecting the capital. Soon they were freely telling her of the military's plans, including one to blockade the Mississippi River. Velazquez spent 13 days in the capital before slipping back across the Potomac River. She reclaimed her Confederate uniform where she had hidden it and reported back as Lieutenant Harry Buford to share the information she had gathered.

Velazquez fought in several battles in Virginia, as well as the siege of Fort Donelson in Tennessee. She was wounded and traveled to New Orleans, hoping to recover before being discovered as a woman. Instead, she was arrested as a spy and imprisoned for 10 days before successfully clearing her name, still without revealing that she was a woman.

She then joined a Louisiana regiment and fought at the Battle of Shiloh along with her husband's close friend Captain De Caulp. The captain had written several letters to Velazquez, and the correspondence had moved from memories of her husband to deeper emotion and finally to a declaration of love. Believing she was still in New Orleans, he had asked her in one of the letters to marry him. He was not aware that Lieutenant Buford, by whose side he fought at Shiloh, was in fact his fiancée. Velazquez was wounded in the battle, and the doctor who treated her discovered she was a woman. She traveled to New Orleans, recovered from her injuries, and then decided to serve the Confederacy in a different way, this time as a female spy.

Velazquez traveled to Cuba and met with Confederate officers living there. She later served as a blockade runner. She was arrested several times, wounded several times, and continued to travel back and forth between Union and Confederate territory, carrying messages and passing on the intelligence she gathered. She assumed numerous disguises, including, again, that of a young Confederate officer.

Velazquez finally met Captain De Caulp, confessed her secret identity to him, and they were married. In her memoir Velazquez claimed that he forbade her from further participation in the war, and that it was not until his death in battle that she resumed her spying. But in fact, De Caulp survived the war and the couple seems to have separated at some point before its end, with Velazquez returning to her work gathering intelligence for the Confederacy.

After the war, Velazquez remarried twice. With her third husband, she traveled extensively through Cuba, Venezuela, and several other Latin American countries. With her fourth husband, a miner, she traveled throughout the American West and died in 1897.

In her memoir, *The Woman in Battle: A Narrative of the Exploits, Adventures, and Travels of Madame Loreta Janeta Velazquez, Otherwise Known as Lieutenant Harry T. Buford, Confederate States Army*, Velazquez offers personal thoughts on the dangerous business of spying in the Civil War. Her words are a fitting picture of all those who served in this conflict by gathering intelligence:

> The position and duties of spies are little understood by persons who have had no actual experience of warfare, and who, consequently, are unable to understand the multitude of agencies it is requisite for the commanders of armies and the heads of governments, which may find it necessary to make an appeal to arms in order to settle their differences, to resort to for the accomplishment of the ends they have in view. Just as the quartermaster, the commissary, the paymaster, and the surgeon are as impor-tant as the generals,—if any fighting worthy of the name is to be done, and warfare is to be an affair of science and skill, instead of a mere trial of brute force,—so the spy, who will be able to obtain information of the movements of the enemy; who will discover the plans for campaigns and battles that are being arranged; who will intercept des-patches; who will carry false intelligence to the enemy, and who, when he does become possessed of any fact worth knowing, will prove himself prompt and reliable in taking it, or sending it to headquarters, is indispensable to the success of any movement.
>
> The spy, however, occupies a different position from that held by any other attaché of an army. According to all military law he is an outlaw, and is liable to be hung if detected—the death of a soldier even being denied him. Nothing has been left undone to render the labors of the spy not only perilous in the extreme, but infamous; and yet the spy is nothing more nor less than a detective of-ficer, and there cannot be any good and sufficient reason assigned for the discredit which attaches to his occupa-tion. It is simply one of the prejudices which, having no substantial foundation, have been carefully fostered by military men for their own purposes, and it is high time that it should be given up by sensible people.

Glossary

ABOLITIONIST   A person seeking to legally end the institution of slavery.

BLOCKADE   A barrier.

BLOCKADE RUNNER   A ship or person that runs through a barrier set up to stop them.

CONFEDERACY   The Southern states that seceded from the United States during the Civil War.

CONFEDERATE ARMY   The army of the South during the Civil War.

CONTRABAND INFORMATION   Information that Union troops obtained from runaway or captured slaves.

GUERRILLA WARFARE   Irregular form of war that involves independent, informal units committing acts of harassment and sabotage.

INTELLIGENCE   Information concerning an enemy or possible enemy's plans or actions.

MILITIA   A group of citizens organized for military service.

SECESSION   The act of breaking away or leaving, as many Southern states did during the period of the Civil War.

UNION ARMY   The army of the North during the Civil War; also called Federal.

UNIONIST   A supporter of the undivided United States; an opponent of Southern state secession.

Bibliography

AmericanCivilWar.com. Available online. URL: http://www.american civilwar.com. Accessed December 8, 2008.

Boyd, Belle. *Belle Boyd in Camp and Prison.* New York: Thomas Yoseloff, 1968.

Burgess, Lauren Cook, ed. *An Uncommon Soldier: The Civil War Letters of Sarah Rosetta Wakeman, alias Private Lyons Wakeman, 153rd Regiment, New York State Volunteers.* Pasadena, Md.: The Minerva Center, 1994.

CivilWarHome.com. "Home of the American Civil War." Available online. URL: http://www.civilwarhome.com. Accessed December 8, 2008.

Duke University Special Collections Library. "Rose O'Neal Greenhow Papers." Available online. URL: http://scriptorium.lib.duke.edu/ greenhow. Accessed December 8, 2008.

Dyer, Thomas G. *Secret Yankees: The Union Circle in Confederate Atlanta.* Baltimore: Johns Hopkins University Press, 1999.

Eby, Cecil D., Jr., ed. *A Virginia Yankee in the Civil War: The Diaries of David Hunter Strother.* Chapel Hill: University of North Carolina Press, 1961.

Feis, William B. *Grant's Secret Service: The Intelligence War from Belmont to Appomattox.* Lincoln: University of Nebraska Press, 2002.

Fishel, Edwin C. *The Secret War for the Union: The Untold Story of Military Intelligence in the Civil War.* Boston: Houghton Mifflin, 1996.

Foote, Shelby. *The Civil War: A Narrative.* New York: Random House, 1958.

Gallman, J. Matthew, ed. *The Civil War Chronicle.* New York: Crown Publishers, 2000.

HarrietTubman.com. Available online. URL: http://www.harriettubman. com. Accessed December 8, 2008.

Haynes, Dennis E. *A Thrilling Narrative: The Memoir of a Southern Unionist.* Fayetteville: University of Arkansas Press, 2006.

Library of Congress. "American Memory." Available online. URL:
    http://memory.loc.gov. Accessed December 8, 2008.

Library of Congress. "America's Story." Available online. URL: http://
    www.americaslibrary.gov. Accessed December 8, 2008.

Massey, Mary Elizabeth. *Women in the Civil War*. Lincoln: University
    of Nebraska Press, 1994.

"Miss Van Lew's Effects," *New York Times*, October 25, 1900. Available
    online. URL: downloaded from nytimes.com.

"Miss Van Lew's Will," *New York Times*, September 30, 1900. Available
    online, URL: downloaded from nytimes.com.

National Library of Medicine, National Institutes of Health. Avail-
    able online. URL: http://www.nlm.nih.gov. Accessed December 8,
    2008.

National Park Service. Available online. URL: http://www.nps.gov. Ac-
    cessed December 8, 20008.

National Public Radio. "Morning Edition." Available online. URL:
    http://www.npr.org/programs/morning. Accessed December 8,
    2008.

Ohio State University Department of History. Available online. URL:
    http://www.ehistory.osu.edu. Accessed December 8, 2008.

Smithsonian Institution. "Civil War @ Smithsonian." Available online.
    URL: http://www.civilwar.si.edu. Accessed December 8, 2008.

Tidwell, William A. *April '65: Confederate Covert Action in the Ameri-
    can Civil War*. Kent, Ohio: Kent State University Press, 1995.

truTV. "Crime Library: Criminal Minds and Methods." Available on-
    line. URL: http://www.crimelibrary.com. Accessed December 8,
    2008.

University of North Carolina Library. "Documenting the American
    South." Available online. URL: http://docsouth.unc.edu. Accessed
    December 8, 2008.

Varon, Elizabeth R. *Southern Lady, Yankee Spy: The True Story of Eliz-
    abeth Van Lew, A Union Agent in the Heart of the Confederacy*.
    New York: Oxford University Press, 2003.

Ward, Geoffrey C. *The Civil War*. New York: Alfred A. Knopf, 1990.

Further Resources

Bolotin, Norman. *Civil War A to Z: A Young Reader's Guide to over 100 People, Places, and Points of Importance*. New York: Dutton, 2002.

Mackay, James. *Allan Pinkerton: The First Private Eye*. New York: Castle Books, 2007.

Stanchak, John. *Civil War*. New York: Dorling Kindersley, 2000.

Taylor, M.W. *Harriet Tubman: Antislavery Activist*. Philadelphia: Chelsea House, 2005.

WEB SITES

American Memory from the Library of Congress
http://memory.loc.gov/ammem/index.html

Civil War Women: Primary Sources on the Internet
http://library.duke.edu/specialcollections/bingham/guides/cwdocs.html

National Geographic Map Machine: Civil War Edition
http://java.nationalgeographic.com/maps/civilwar

National Park Service, The American Civil War Homepage
http://cwar.nps.gov/civilwar

The Papers of Jefferson Davis
http://jeffersondavis.rice.edu

The University of North Carolina Library: Documenting the American South
http://docsouth.unc.edu

University of Virginia Library American Civil War Collection
http://etext.lib.virginia.edu/civilwar

Picture Credits

Index

About the Authors

HEATHER LEHR WAGNER is a writer and editor. She earned a master's degree in government from the College of William and Mary and a bachelor's degree in political science from Duke University. She is the author of more than 40 books exploring political and social issues, including *The Outbreak of the Civil War* in the MILESTONES IN AMERICAN HISTORY series.

TIM MCNEESE is associate professor of history at York College in York, Nebraska, where he is in his seventeenth year of college instruction. Professor McNeese earned an associate of arts degree from York College, a bachelor of arts in history and political science from Harding University, and a master of arts in history from Missouri State University. A prolific author of books for elementary, middle school, high school, and college readers, McNeese has published more than 100 books and educational materials over the past 20 years, on everything from the founding of early New York to Hispanic authors. His writing has earned him a citation in the library reference work *Contemporary Authors* and multiple citations in *Best Books for Young Teen Readers*. In 2006, McNeese appeared on the History Channel program *Risk Takers, History Makers: John Wesley Powell and the Grand Canyon*. He was a faculty member at the 2006 Tony Hillerman Writers Conference in Albuquerque. His wife, Beverly, is an assistant professor of English at York College. They have two married children, Noah and Summer, and three grandchildren, Ethan, Adrianna, and Finn William. Tim and Bev McNeese sponsored study trips for college students on the Lewis and Clark Trail in 2003 and 2005 and to the American Southwest in 2008. You may contact Professor McNeese at tdmcneese@york.edu.